All Families Matters

The Black Redemptive

CHRISTINE AINER,
M.DIV., D.MIN.

SWEETSPIRE **LITERATURE**
—— MANAGEMENT ——

This work is dedicated to my Lord and God Jesus Christ
Who is the head of my life, and to my husband and family,
who has enriched my life through every season of life.

All glory be unto God.

Preface

The relationship between the black man and the black woman has been negatively impacted and affected by society. Stressors such as underemployment and unemployment are a couple of factors that has directed the success or destruction of the relationship. If much of your time must be used wondering how to succeed financially it can negatively affect the intimacy in a marriage. The lack of intimacy in a couple's relationship can cause conflict. The struggle and suffering from societal oppression, mistreatment, and disadvantage has led to a decline in black marriages and black families as if it doesn't matter. But the bottom line is All families matter to God. That means you matter individually as well as collectively and should treat each other as if you matter. Our family must first matter to us if we are to expect it to matter to anyone else. Intense unresolved family conflict is not conducive to the black redemptive. Loving God while loving one another, loving the family while walking in unity with God will defeat evil systems, this is the black redemptive. "In the Citation by Edmondson, Mika, "Unearned Suffering Is Redemptive: the Roots and Implications of Martin Luther King, Jr's Redemptive Suffering Theodicy", King held that persons have the freedom and responsibility to agapically engage their suffering to help bring about personal and social transformation." (Mika Edmondson, Calvin Theological Seminary, 2017) Although Dr. King is declaring a source of hope and strength the church has in conflict and battle against the injustice in this world, I believe we can also apply it to the conflict in families, individually and collectively, because you are the church. We must cooperate with Jesus as we relate to one another in the building up of our families. Our relationships with one another in our homes should model the compassion of Christ. This means leaning into Jesus as we press our way through difficult times in our marriage and family. This will take some selfless longsuffering, but it can be done if we heed to God's instructions that tells us, "However, each one of you also must love his wife as he loves himself, and the wife must respect her husband." (NIV)

Although society still has a responsibility to reduce racial inequities, still we are not at the mercy of society for hope. There is hope in the plans of God. God want us to walk according to his will first and foremost.

- His will is unity in the family.
- His will is Cooperation not competition.
- His will is forgiving not blaming each other in the family.
- His will is Respect not disrespect in your family.
- His will is to value your family and not to underestimate each other in your family. Your "family matter" and it starts with you.

CHAPTER 1

History of the Relationship of the Black Man and Black Woman

Because of societal pressure, the relationship between the black man and the black woman has been, for a most part, destructive. Although we must admit that the issues of racism, unemployment, poverty, and housing, among many other things, have caused a great problem in the black family, the fact remains that there is hope for the black man and the black woman's relationship to go from destructive to redemptive.

I believe the history of the black man must be taken into consideration before we can clearly understand why the rift exists in the relationship between the black man and the black woman.

It has been over 159 years since slavery was abolished. Yet the effects of slavery have been lingering since 1865 when it was ratified and formalized. The black man and woman have been taught division from slavery until now by the society they found themselves in.

During slavery, the women were forced to have babies by their masters. Their masters regarded them as common personal property; thus, they exploited them and the children they produced for financial gain. Families were divided purposely to keep them from bonding, loving, unifying, and gaining power. In an effort to survive in a cruel social system, division grew between the house slaves and field slaves. According to James E. Blackwell, "The most important status distinctions stemmed from the occupational stratification of Blacks as either house slaves (for instance, serving as maids, butlers, cooks, nursemaids, coachmen, laundry workers, and companions) or as field slaves (performing non roles on the plantation such as that of a field hand)" (Blackwell 1975). The division between house slaves and field slaves was huge. One was thought of as higher than the other. In other words, the house slaves thought they were better than the field slaves, and as a result, some supplied derogatory information on other slaves to pull down those slaves to get points for themselves. This divisive behavior can still be found to this day in many relationships in the black community. Division brings destruction. In Mark 3:25, Jesus says, "And if a house is divided against itself, that house will not be able to stand."

Today blacks are not directly forced to have babies: however, some have had babies for economic survival, to receive a welfare check, food stamps, and low-incoming housing while the black fathers and husbands are locked up on the modern-day slave plantation called the state prison system, where they still have a slave master called a warden, who tell them when to eat, sleep, etc. As it is reported in the TribLive Opinion, Obama sees racism in the incarceration rate: "We have certain sentences that are based less on the kind of crime you commit than on what you look like and where you come from." Indeed, in 2006, blacks, who are less than 13 percent of the population, were 37.5 percent of all state and federal prisoners. About one in 33 black men was in prison, compared with one in 79 Hispanic men and one in 205 white men." (Will 2008). Statistics proves that black men shifted from one type of slavery to another. Many have been socialized in a system that taught them to continue in a slave mentality. Many have been marginalized, institutionalized, disabled, hardened, and living in survival mode. Thus, those that found themselves caught up in this maze have not been available nor able to effectively be accountable for their families.

The black man and black woman have been taught division from the very beginning of their arrival in America until now. To keep bread on the table and a roof over their heads, many have relied on the system to support them because of the lack of opportunities to find substantial employment. To survive, some black women has found themselves applying for public assistance, sometimes this meant that the black man had to remove himself from the home, giving up his right as provider and protector of his family.

When I grew up in the South, I noticed that it was a common thing for the black man to leave his family behind to go north or become a Merchant Marine or go elsewhere to find work to take care of his family. He would either come home for quick visits, or if he was able to make enough money, he could sometimes send for his family to relocate with him. To financially provide for the family, absenteeism took place. Many of the women had to be the ones to leave and go north to work as housekeepers and send the money back home to feed the families and to survive. Some of these women went to school and got degrees and/or trades and obtained better jobs. And since they were not seen to be as much of a threat as the black man, they were promoted and sometimes promotion caused them to become indirect competitors with their black men instead of supporters of their black men. Unfortunately, this can lead some men to feel inadequate.

For many black men, depression and a fear of failure set in, as well as a lack of motivation to try to excel. Yet, this is not the black woman's fault. The black woman has played an important part in the building up and the motivating of the black man.

Since the arrival of the black man and the black woman on the slave ship, there has been some division in the family. The purpose for bringing them here was not to build happy and healthy black families; instead, the purpose was to use and abuse each one of them and keep them divided. It was never intended for them to have a life together to raise children and teach them how to love and live in unity, because this was not economically conducive to the business owner. And yes, that is exactly what the black man and black woman were used for—business only. They were considered a commodity.

As a result, many homes have had no male figure in the home; instead, they have been headed up by black females. This has caused many male children to view the female as the strong provider in the home, and there has been confusion in the male children about who is the leader of the household because many of them have never seen strong male leadership because of the male absenteeism in the home, leaving the female to lead the household.

Young black men benefit from a strong male role model, a mentor, a father figure to encourage him and teach him what it is to be a man. The reason some men don't mind letting the woman continue taking care of them is because many of them have seen their mothers, aunts, and grandmothers provide for the households, and this is the model they are comfortable receiving. Although the mother/woman of the house is strong and loving, she can never take the place of a strong godly male figure in the home.

Amid trying to survive, it is wise for the black man and the black woman to take the time to take another look at the broad view of what is continuing to happen to them and their families in America. A survival mode attitude must end if we are going to ever get on the right track of building families in the way God intended for families to be constructed. It is time to stop, regroup, and get back to the word and will of God.

CHAPTER 2

God's Divine Purpose
for the Black Man
and Woman

Genesis chapter 1 is the unfolding of God's eternal purpose for man. When God (the Father) said, "Let us make man in our image", he was saying he made all humans to resemble and represent him and have dominion over every other creation in His name, because we did not evolve from other lower forms of life (Gen. 1:26-28). All humans of every race, color and nationality were created in the likeness of God with the capacity to rule over creation and be in relationship with God, other humans, and to exercise choice, and moral consciousness. When reading the opening verses of Genesis, one can get the idea that God is designing and creating a habitable place of importance for someone. And that someone is man. And yes, the black man is included. This means that he was created in the image of God. Not in the image of a slave master or animals. Yet he fell into the hands of his first slave master—the serpent, the deceiver, the carnal one.

There is no freedom from the side effects of modern-day slavery until there is freedom from the first slave master, which is the serpent. True freedom comes from the blood of Jesus Christ, who is the image of the invisible God, the firstborn of every creature. See Colossians 1:14. Our relationship with God can build a loving and trusting relationship with each other. We can get the strength to bear productive fruit by growing in the knowledge of God, which is conducive for lasting relationships to take place. Colossians 1:11–13 tells us, "Strengthened with all might according to his glorious power, unto all patience and longsuffering with joyfulness, who has delivered us from the power of darkness, and hath translated us into the kingdom of his dear Son."

God has given a solution that cannot be replaced, and it is the prescription for the healing that is needed to bring black families into a productive relationship. When each one submits to the Son of God and allows Him to heal and restore their relationship, then unity will take place but until that time there will be division and discord. Those who surrender to God's instructions find peace in unity. Marriage wins when the marriage is a triangle. Husband, wife, and God at the head.

The Adam and Eve Disorder

Adam was told to be the leader and to follow the lead of his Father, God; instead, he followed Eve as Eve followed the serpent. The question is why would Adam and Eve disobey God and fall into such destruction?

- Was it because Adam paid more attention to his wife than to the spiritual things of God?
- Was it because he idolized Eve's beauty more than he loved God.

Moreover, Genesis 2:17 tells us that God instructed Adam that he was not to eat of the tree of the knowledge of good and evil because if he did, he would surely die. Before God made Eve, Adam was aware of the consequence of disobeying his maker. Adam was the head of the woman and was supposed to protect her and be responsible for her. He was also supposed to communicate to her what God had told him. The woman did not quote what was quoted to Adam. Though speculative, I believe it is safe to say that Adam did not make himself clear about what God had said to him. As a matter of fact, Adam thought so little of what God had instructed him that he followed Eve in the eating from the tree himself which reveals not taking the responsibility of the command God gave to him.
(Rom.5:12-14; 1 Tim. 2:14)

There is a great need for the black man to take responsibility for his life and his family by obeying God first and not his wife. This is not to say that he shouldn't discuss and communicate with his wife and have consideration for his wife's input, but it does mean that he must understand that he cannot put his responsibility of making final decisions on his wife and still be in order with God, and expect to be respected by his wife. It is time to understand that his first responsibility is to God and that he must obey God. The blessing of God comes through seeking and obeying God and following His instructions. Man will have to have a love for God that exceeds the love that he has for woman.

Man must humble himself and submit to God to learn from God what it is God wants him to do. And as a black man that has been abused and exploited in a hostile society, he must realize that he must forgive those who abused and exploited him and then realize that he is "fearfully and wonderfully" made, and that he can succeed as a man of God, father, and husband and receive his deliverance from the side effects of slavery.

One of the side effects of slavery is embedded anger and unforgiveness. When there is embedded anger and unforgiveness plaguing a person, it is toxic to the person spiritually. Anger grieves the Holy Spirit. For victory to take place, he must forgive the ones who oppressed him in this society and take charge of his life in the Holy Spirit. As it is revealed in Ephesians 4:31–32, "Let all bitterness, and wrath, and anger, and clamor, and evil speaking, be put away from you, along with all malice: And be ye kind one to another, tenderhearted, forgiving one another, even as God for Christ's sake hath forgiven you."

Anger grieves the Holy Spirit. For victory to take place, he must forgive the ones who oppressed him in this society and take charge of his life in the Holy Spirit. Forgiveness is not a weakness; it is a strength.

Surrender and submission to Christ Jesus as Savior and Lord is vitally important. Adam knew God, yet he did not submit to the authority of God. When we submit to the authority of God and stop rebelling against His will for our life, we will see the blessings of God flowing through order and obedience. The more we seek him, the more we will know his will.

Jesus said, "But seek ye first the kingdom of God and His righteousness; and all these things shall be added unto you" (Matt. 6:33). God wants you to look to Him and depend on Him for everything in your life, having a desire for His righteous rule in your life.

Reflection

1. Read Acts 17:26 and tell what this has to do with you.

_____

_____

_____

_____

_____

_____

2. Read Galatians 3:28 and tell what this means in reference to you.

_____

_____

_____

_____

_____

_____

3. Study Genesis 9:18–19 and discuss.

_____

_____

_____

_____

_____

_____

4. Read Deuteronomy 5:32 and discuss how you can be assured of living a prosperous and blessed life.

_____

_____

_____

_____

_____

5. Study 1 John 2:15–17 and state how you are to view the world.

_____

_____

_____

_____

_____

6. Read Ephesians 4:32 and state the requirements for you.

_____

_____

_____

_____

_____

_____

7. Read 2 Corinthians 2:7–10 and memorize how to reaffirm your love.

_____

_____

_____

_____

_____

_____

8. Read Mark 11:25–26 and state the means of our forgiveness.

_____

_____

_____

_____

_____

_____

9. Read 1 John 1:9 and state how to experience spiritual cleansing.

_____

_____

_____

_____

_____

_____

CHAPTER 3

The Effects of Anger

Misplaced revenge is destructive.

- The redemptive process will take place in the relationship between the black man and the black woman when they stop using each other for a sounding board and taking out their frustrations on one another. It is time to turn to the only one that can take the misplaced aggression from you and deposit love in you that covers a multitude of sins. First Peter 4:8 tells us, "Above all, keep fervent in your love for one another, because love covers a multitude of sins." Proverbs 10:12 tells us, "Hatred stirs up quarrels, but love covers all offenses" (NAS).

This means that we are to live our entire lives according to God's will and not human desires. Even though "love covers a multitude of sin," it does not ignore, overlook, or try to hide sin.

The "covering of sins" is a gift of God that believers have. We can forgive one another because Christ has forgiven us. The Love of Christ works as a shock absorber, cushioning and smoothing out the bumps and irritations caused by others (*Life Application New Testament Commentary* 2001) The first thing the black man and black woman must do is rest in Christ, who is the only one who can truly love. The love of Christ will heal relationships. One must be saved to truly love, because the flesh is not capable of love. When love takes place, hatred and bitterness will die. But everyone needs a role model of love before they can love, and this may not be found in a dysfunctional family suffering from abuse and exploitation. However, thanks be to God that He is the perfect role model and that is where we should look. John 3:16a tells us, "For God so loved the world that He gave His only begotten Son." This means love is sacrifice. For the redemptive process in the relationship between the black man and the black woman to take place, sacrifice must take place in their relationships.

Love Is Sacrifice!

First Corinthians 13 tells us what love is and what love is not.

- Love is patient.
- Love is kind.
- Love is not jealous.
- Love does not brag.
- Love is not arrogant.
- Love does not act unbecomingly.
- Love does not seek its own.
- Love is not provoked.
- Love does not take into account a wrong suffered.
- Love does not rejoice in unrighteousness.
- Love rejoices with the truth.
- Love bears all things, believes all things, hopes all things, endures all things, and love never fails.

In other words, love is a winner!

Hebrews 12:14–15 instructs us, "Follow peace with all men, and holiness, without which no man shall see the Lord." Verse 15 says, "Looking diligently lest any man fail of the grace of God; lest any root of bitterness springing up trouble you, and thereby many be defiled."

God's holy word is telling us that when we hold on to anger and nurture it and feed it, there will be negative growth—growth in the wrong direction. When bitterness takes place, this is negative growth, and it will cause double trouble in relationships. If you let the devil put you on this anger detour, it will be trouble for you before it becomes trouble for anyone else, because it is the devil's detour to keep you so angry you cannot think straight enough to plan for a productive future. This is not intended to be a blanket statement because there are some who have allowed the Lord to show them the way out of the devil's maze. Yet there are many black men and women who are still suffering from the dis-ease of anger and losing their talents to anger. That is why many of them are not pursuing employment or going into business for themselves. It is possible to lose hope if your application for employment, housing, and loans are too often turned down. This can cause one to become temperamental. A temperamental person is liable to change in mood.

I have ministered to many young black men and women who are extremely intelligent, yet they are wasting away from anger and depression. Many of them state that they feel as if they are trapped in this world with talents that cannot be used. But this is a lie from the devil. It is a chain reaction set in motion by the devil to keep them and their families divided. Many have set out on the devil's detour of using their talents for crime, such as drug dealing, which leads to slavery and prison. The detour and trap of drug dealing and drug taking is another form of slavery set up to keep one group of people materially rich and one group poor, depressed, oppressed, and disabled. When we depend solely on the world system for empowerment and satisfaction, we will obey rules that are carnal. When you build up the carnal man, you will be more prone to holding on to anger. When someone allows anger to grow into bitterness, they become intoxicated by it. They become poisoned by it, and stinking in their thinking, and stinking thinking can bring about stinking actions.

When someone is addicted to anger, that person has learned to operate under the influence of anger. This may have become the only way that that person knows how to communicate. When anyone gets stuck in such a survival mode he or she will be on the defensive all the time, trying to survive in being right, trying to survive in feeling better about themselves. Every morning when he or she gets up, he or she must get a dose of anger to survive, because he or she has become stuck, and it has become a habit to talk and act a certain way and he or she is not comfortable acting any other way.

Have you ever seen a person that is just cranky all the time? Have you ever seen a person for whom you know you must think about how to fix what you have to say before you say it because you know he or she is like a stick of dynamite all the time?

As the scripture tells us, bitterness is a root. When I think about a root, I realize that a root is hidden deep down in something. Before anger can take root, it must be watered and fed and fertilized. When you continue to bring up the past mistakes that your significant other made and when you are determined to revisit your past hurts, you are watering your anger with unforgiveness and resentment and hatred and anxiety and premeditation of how you are going to get someone back. You are then allowing bitterness to take root. And soon disaster will follow.

Then the bitterness that has taken root will get stronger and stronger, and you must do something to quiet it down, and at this point depression may set in. Now you need something to keep you from going over the edge in your depression. So many will begin to take antidepressant pills and alcohol and street drugs and sex and food addictions and anything else carnal they can get their minds and hands on to ease the pain that comes from that deep-seated root of bitterness, unforgiveness, resentment, and jealousy.

It is destructive to retaliate and take revenge. When we are hurt, we are tempted to hurt back. Many times, those who had nothing to do with the cause of the anger can be hurt. It is time to break the cycle. It is time to say, "I will not live like this any longer." It is time to say, "I will be the one to make the change, even though I may believe the other person is more at fault than I am." How else can we take the words of Jesus when he said, "Bless them that curse you and pray for them which despitefully use you" (Luke 6:28 KJV). The Bible says, "Not rendering evil for evil, or railing for railing: but contrariwise blessing; knowing that ye are thereunto called, that ye should inherit a blessing" (1 Pet. 3:9). When you do this, you will reverse the cycle. The apostle Paul said in Romans 12:17–18, "Recompense to no man evil for evil. Provide things honest in the sight of all men. If it be possible, as much as lieth in you, live peaceably with all men." Doing as God has instructed in the Holy Scriptures will bring a blessing and healing to your life and your family life.

It is time for the rage and bitterness and every other dysfunction that is hindering the black man from a redemptive relationship with his family to stop and reverse. It is time to say, enough is enough. We will not allow the sins and sickness of past generations to affect our families and homes. There will be no abuse of any kind here, physical, sexual, or verbal. There will be no name-calling here. There will be no unfaithfulness here. The abuse of alcohol and drugs will find no place in our homes or our lives. There will be no abuse of time in our lives. We will be the ones to start businesses, even if others in our extended families decide not to. You can break the cycle and be a positive role model by being the first one to start a business, produce a product and provide for your family.

At some point, the patterns of past generations must be broken. Determine that you and your family will be the ones to break the curse. Your family will be redemptive as you bless each other and give worth to each other. Your family will be the beginning of a godly line, the beginning of a new generation that will produce healthy and productive people who will be a blessing to future generations.

The cure is surrender and submission to Christ Jesus as Savior, Lord, and ruler of your life. Adam knew God, yet he did not submit to the authority of God, and that is why he failed. Adam broke the relationship he had with God when he disobeyed God. He showed his independence from God in the act of making his own decision. When we make decisions independent of God, we are self-focus, and self-centered and self-determined, and self-destructive. In John 15:5 the bible says, "Apart from me you can do nothing".

The Bible says, "For where envying and strife is, there is confusion and every evil work" (James 3:16). Dysfunction in the family, or on a personal level, comes when we put ourselves first. (Phil. 2:3). Adam put himself first when he decided to follow and obey Eve and the serpent instead of God. He disregarded his allegiance to God. Again, we are always better off seeking God's will first and acting according to it. When Adam followed his own will he became a servant of the serpent instead of a servant of God.

We should participate with God and become God's servants to receive the best He has for us. If we become servants of the serpent instead of servants of God anger will set forth to destroy our families. We can't produce any valuable fruit in our lives if we have bitter roots, unrepented anger becomes rooted in sin.

According to the discourse of John C. Rankin, on the "Serpents Original Agenda, the curse, Cain and his Lineage: A Remarkable Observation in the Hebrew Text, the ancient serpent first appears with an angry agenda against the woman, this anger transfers to the man, then to Cain and then to his lineage." He further states the consequences are devastating, and for which we all need the Savior. (John C. Rankin, December 3, 2018)

Reflection

Study Galatians 5:17–26. Examine yourself. According to the scriptures, what fruit are you missing that will be beneficial to you, your spouse, and your family as a whole?

_____

_____

_____

_____

_____

_____

KINGDOM PEOPLE RESEMBLE THE KING

Jesus said it very simply in Luke 17:21, "The kingdom of God is within you." The Pharisees were so self-centered and so self-righteous that they did not understand that the kingdom was already among them because it had arrived in Jesus Christ. Those who have given their life to Christ have the kingdom within and are also waiting for the full expression of that kingdom when Jesus comes back that they may be moved into His fullness. Anyone turned against Gods children are turned against God and must be born again to operate as a kingdom child. Those who are allowing the kingdom of God to reflect in and through them will be able to reflect the fruit of the Spirit of God. This brings us to an important question: what kingdom do you choose to allow to be within you? If you reflect the Spirit of God, it comes from the Kingdom of God within. If you reflect the kingdom of Hell, the kingdom of Hell is within, and you must be born again, or you will spend eternity in the kingdom that you are representing. If you choose to habitually fashion your character in the wrong way, which is obeying the flesh, you will not get the kingdom blessing. In John 8:31, Jesus said, "You shall know the truth and the truth shall make you free." If anyone want to know the truth, that person must get to know Jesus. And when they get to know Jesus, they will find that they are not bound by political institutions or by intellectual knowledge. The side effects of slavery cannot keep you bounded if you surrender your life and everything about your life to Jesus Christ.

CHAPTER 4

It Is Time to Switch Masters

Black Americans came from Africa in chains. They were used in a most gruesome way. Uncared for, unloved, divided, beaten, starved, killed, and totally deprived of everything—yet they have not been annihilated. By the grace of God, the black race is still here and there is a purpose for them.

There are many black men and black women that left legacies of surviving by leaving a track record for being steadfast, immovable, and abounding in the Lord. Frederick Douglass is just one of many that leaned on the Lord to succeed. Even during the most difficult times for the black man, Frederick Douglass did not throw in the towel and give up. When it was illegal for a black man to read and write, Douglass did not allow that to be an obstacle to him. He became a learned man by making a conscious decision to educate himself with that which was constructive and productive. He switched masters by not allowing the plantation owner to fix his destiny. He became a Christian and taught himself to read the Bible. He switched masters when he found out who God was and what God would do if he believed in him and obeyed him. He persevered through the gruesome trials and tribulations that were part of his everyday life. Because he persevered, he was able to rise to great success. Some of his accomplishments are as follows:

- He was an ordained minister of the African Methodist Episcopal Church.
- He was a United States marshal.
- He was the recorder of deeds for the District of Columbia.
- He was Haiti's commissioner to the Chicago World's Columbian Exposition.
- In 1872, Douglass became the very first African American nominated as a vice presidential candidate in the US. At the 1888 Republican National Convention, Douglass became the first African American to receive a vote for president of the United States in a major party's roll call vote.
- He was an editor of many newspapers.
- He was an author of numerous books.
- He was a renowned orator.
- He was a husband and a father.

(http://en.wikipedia.org/wiki/Frederick Douglass.)

Here was a black man living during the worst times for black people. He literally had to fight with the dogs and cats for the scraps from the table and for the crumbs that were shaken off the tablecloth. Yet he did not allow his circumstances to dictate his success. I believe that Douglass, Tubman, Sojourner, and many others are great role models for the black man and black woman today, in that if they were able to be a success when they were not even allowed to go to school, You certainly can get an education and be a success too. Don't be fooled by the devil. You can make it in life. You can provide for your family. You are important to God. But you must unite with those who want to do the right thing. And most importantly, you must be united with God through Jesus Christ and filled with the Holy Spirit.

Frederick Douglass's favorite quote was, "I would unite with anybody to do right and with nobody to do wrong" (http://en.wikipedia.org/wiki/Fredrick Douglass). The only way that you can possibly do right is to unite with the Lord. When you unite with the Lord, the Lord becomes your master, and no matter how bad a situation may look, the master is in control, and you will be victorious. One of Fredrick Douglass best quotes were, "One and God make a majority".

- You don't have to be enslaved to the sin of bitterness and unforgiveness.
- You don't have to be enslaved to the past.
- You don't have to be enslaved to fear, doubt, unbelief, etc.

You are enslaved to that which you obey. Whatever or whomever you recognize as having control over you is your master. If you obey the commands of sin, then sin is your master. If you obey the commands of righteousness, then righteousness is your master, and you will experience freedom and eternal life.

In Romans 6:15–16, Paul tells us, "What then? Shall we sin because we are not under the law but grace? May it never be! Do you not know that when you present yourselves to someone as slaves of the one whom you obey, either of sin resulting in death, or of obedience resulting in righteousness?" Paul is telling us that it is up to us to make the choice in the yielding of our members. There are only two choices of whom you yield your members to:

Choice 1: Walk in rebellion, which is a slave to sin
Choice 2: Walk in righteousness

When Fredrick Douglas switched masters he didn't become a hermit, he had friends and associates. But they were not his idol nor master of his life. For the most part they had the same agenda. It's good to have friends who will be a positive motivation. Friends that will build you up and not tear you down. Friends that want to live for the Lord and will hold you accountable can be a great influence. Friends that identify with the Lord will not expect you to idolize them. Identify with the Master, Jesus, and then to positive role models in the family, church, and the community. The bible tells us, "Neither be ye called masters: for one is your Master, even Christ." (KJV)

Productive progress is made in our earthly relationships when we allow Jesus to be Master over of our relationships, speech, decisions, marriage, family, careers, and everything in our life. This happens when we surrender everything to him. In 1 Corinthians 2:14–15, Paul tells us, "But the natural man receiveth not the things of the Spirit of God: for they are foolishness unto him: neither can he know them because they are spiritually discerned." The natural and spiritual man are in direct opposition to one another.

The only way you are going to be a winner at anything is to be in harmony with God by being in his will. You will not accomplish the best that God has for you if you insist on being linked up with your natural side more so than your spiritual side. For the spiritual man is being led and directed by God and the natural man by the flesh. It is good to assess and evaluate what you are speaking into your life and into your family's lives. It is not productive to let negative words /unwise talk master your life. It is up to you to switch from the master of sin to the master of freedom and life. You can speak freedom from sin. You can speak radiant health, riches, safety, and whatever else the scriptures promise you. Proverbs 10:19–20 tells us, "In the multitude of words there wanteth not sin: but he that refrained his lips is wise. The tongue of the just is as choice silver; the heart of the wicked is little worth." God guards our words if they are correct. The Bible says in 1 Samuel 3:19, "And Samuel grew, and the Lord was with him and did not let any of his words fall to the ground." Words spoken in harmony with the will of God for your life will be blessed and not destructive. If you walk in righteousness, you will present your body as a living sacrifice—this includes your tongue—to the Lord for His use and for His glory. The choice is yours; you can serve whomever you want. Remember, there is an outcome for serving each master: one is death and bondage; the other is life and freedom in Christ Jesus.

In Romans 6:19, Paul tells us, "I am speaking in human terms because of the weakness of your flesh. For just as you presented your members as slaves to impurity and to lawlessness, resulting in further lawlessness, so now present your members as slaves to righteousness, resulting in sanctification." Paul is telling us not to push the details of slavery too far. He is using an illustration so we can understand the concept being taught. You are not slaves to God in the sense that you have no freedom of choice. It is to be understood by you that if you choose to serve Him, you will receive many blessings. All the promises of God's word belong to you when you serve Him in love and obedience. If you give yourself to sin, you will get more sin. But if you give yourself to Christ, you will become more like Christ.

Reflection

1. Paul tells us in Romans 6:15–23 that we have the right to surrender our bodies to a master. Based on what master you are serving right now, which master have you switched from and how did you switch masters and when did you switch masters?

   _____

   _____

   _____

   _____

2. Read Ephesians 2:1–3 and discuss your life before you switched masters.

   _____

   _____

   _____

   _____

   _____

   _____

   _____

   _____

3. Read 2 Corinthians 5:17. What happens once we have surrendered to Jesus Christ?

_____

_____

_____

_____

_____

_____

_____

Jesus went to the slave market and purchased our freedom from being slaves to sin.

4. Revelation 5:9 tells us that Jesus _____ us.
5. In Galatians 4:5, the word "redeem" means "to buy in the market and remove from sale."
6. In 1 Peter 1:18–19, the word "redeemed" means to recover after the payment of a ransom price. It means a slave that has been purchased in the market and set free. In context this is about Jesus paying the price for our freedom from hell. But also after we receive salvation we are no longer enslaved to the carnal ways of getting relief.

Do not become enslaved to your tongue.

Read and study the following scriptures and discuss the meaning:

- Proverbs 21:23 _____
  _____
  _____

- Proverbs 12:25 _____
  _____
  _____

- Proverbs 18:6–8 _____
  _____
  _____

- Proverbs 18:20 _____
  _____
  _____

- Proverbs 18:21 _____
  _____
  _____

- Ephesians 4:29 _____
  _____
  _____

- Ephesians 5:4 _____
  _____
  _____

- Mark 11:23 _____

  _____

  _____

- James 3:8-11 _____

  _____

  _____

- Philippians 4:8 _____

  _____

  _____

CHAPTER 5

Let Go of Vengeance

God knows that you have been discriminated against and oppressed.

The Bible says in Jeremiah 51:11, "Make the arrows bright! Gather the shields! The Lord has raised up the spirit of the kings of the Medes. For His plan is against Babylon to destroy it, because it is the vengeance of the Lord, the vengeance for His temple" (NKJV). What the Lord is saying here is He has not forgotten how Babylon has fiercely abused Israel. The Lord states that he will repay Babylon. That is why you should never take vengeance on your own. God knows who, what, and why one is being oppressed and another is being the oppressor. At one time He used Babylon as the "battle ax" for judgment against Judah, and another time He would stretch his hand against Babylon and crumble them by His power forever (Jer. 51:20–26). No one will get away with their evil deeds. Everyone will reap what they sow.

God is not only the God of love; He is the God of vengeance too.

The vengeance of God is about balancing the scales of right and wrong, retribution, punishment, and bringing justice.

Vengeance is God's response to sin, wickedness, and rebellion. God is righteous, and it is His right as well as His duty to punish the wicked. How can a holy and righteous God overlook wickedness? He will not be untrue to His character of holiness and justice. Nahum1:3 says, "The Lord is slow to anger and great in power; the LORD will not leave the guilty unpunished" (NAS). Proverbs 11:21 also says, "Be sure of this: The wicked will not go unpunished, but those who are righteous will go free." God is not only a God of vengeance; he is also a God of mercy to those who repent of their sinful, wicked ways.

The mercy of God is beyond man's imagination. In Psalm 116:5, the psalmist says, "Gracious is the LORD, and righteous; yea, our God is merciful" God wants to love you and pour out His kindness and compassion upon you. It is His will that you live a life walking in His will and His way, not in the way of sin.

It is you who causes the hand of wrath or vengeance to come down on you when you choose to live a life of sin and disobedience. Second Peter 3:9 says, "The Lord is not slow in keeping his promise, as some understand slowness, He is patient with you, not wishing anyone to perish, but for everyone to come to repentance" (NAS). He is so merciful; he will wait a long time for you to come into repentance so that you can enjoy a life that is the fullness of joy. You cannot enjoy a life of fullness unless you have the Holy Spirit dwelling in you and filling you. You cannot let go of vengeance unless you have surrendered your life to Him totally. We can find full expression of God's mercy, love, and grace nowhere else but at the cross of Jesus. Jesus is the perfect sacrifice for your sin.

Why would you ever want to take any vengeance in your own hands when you could not ever repay your oppressor in a lasting way as God could? That is why you should let go of all vengeance today and understand that the big payback is on the agenda to take place in God's timing. You are called to walk in love and forgivingness.

The Bible says in Hebrews 10:30–31, "For we know him that hath said, vengeance belongeth unto me, I will recompense, saith the Lord. And again, The Lord shall judge his people. It is a fearful thing to fall into the hands of the living God." That is why you should never try to get even with those who you think have wronged you because when you do, you remove the room for God's wrath. You have taken things into your own hands, and now the other person may not experience the fullness of what God has for them because of your interference. In Romans 12:17–19, Paul says,

"Never pay back evil for evil to anyone. Respect what is right in the sight of all men. If possible, so far as it depends on you, be at peace with all men. Never take your own revenge, beloved, but leave room for the wrath of God, for it is written, *'Vengeance is mine, I will repay,'* says the Lord."

- Are you holding a grudge against someone? What can you do to help them grow?
- Do you want to get even or get someone back? Turn it over to God for payment.
- Are you saying, "I will get them back for holding me back or mistreating me or stealing from me?" Let it go and repent. Don't miss your blessing. If you want your trespasses forgiven, you must forgive those who have trespassed against you.

Everyone who does injustice and evil to another will not go unpunished by God. You should let it go and give it to God and He will punish the wicked. You don't have to worry about them getting away. The one and only true and living God is not ignorant.

He is Omnipotent (Jer. 32:17, 27), Omnipresent (Ps.139:7– 12), and Omniscient (1 John 3:20).

Reflection

1. Read Jeremiah chapters 50 and 51 and discuss the Babylonians and state in your own words how this applies to you and your situation.

_____

_____

_____

_____

2. Some have the idea that they should not allow anyone to run over them. So, they have the idea that if you hit me, I'm going to hit you back, and I'm going to hit you twice as hard as you hit me because I want to win the fight. Some think that is the way to win a fight.

Read Matthew 5:38–48 and discuss what this means to you.

_____

_____

_____

_____

How can you consistently do this?

_____

_____

_____

_____

_____

_____

_____

Remember God never sleeps or slumbers.

Second Chronicles 16:9 tells you that the Lord will show himself strong on behalf of whom and why?

_____

_____

_____

_____

_____

_____

What does Psalm 149 tells you to do anyway!

_____

_____

_____

Micah 5:15 says God is the one who executes.

_____

_____

_____

Luke 6:37 tells you forgive and

_____

_____

_____

_____

Read Matthew 18:21–22 and discuss: if your brother sins against you, what should you do?

_____

_____

_____

_____

_____

_____

_____

_____

_____

Proverbs 26:27 tells you that it is dangerous to

_____

_____

_____

_____

_____

_____

_____

First Peter 3:12, the encouragement in this passage is

_____

_____

_____

_____

_____

_____

_____

_____

CHAPTER 6

The Danger of Anger

Ephesians 4:26–27 says, "Be ye angry, and sin not; let not the sun go down upon your wrath: Neither give place to the devil."

Admitting to anger and dealing with anger in a constructive way is good. Relationships can be destroyed when anger is not expressed in constructive ways. The Scriptures encourages us to get angry appropriately. It warns us not to hold a grudge. It urges us to strive to forgive each other, to be kind to one another.

One constructive way to handle anger is to write a letter to the other person in the relationship, expressing how you feel.

Holding on to anger can be dangerous. Notice, anger is one letter from danger.

- Dangerous anger made Cain kill Abel.
- Dangerous anger made Saul lose his throne and eventually his life.
- Dangerous anger made Moses smite the rock and miss the promised land.

We were all created with basic human emotions, and anger is one of them. However, it is one that includes hostility that can turn people against each other.

Anger can become dangerous when it is repressed. Repressing your anger is a process of burying it within and ignoring that it exists. And it accumulates in what I call a toxic dump bank. The more it accumulates, the more explosive it becomes, until one day it does explode.

The important point to remember is that when anger is not met with a biblical solution, you can end up killing yourself or someone else. Inappropriate or destructive anger is a killer. If destructive anger does not kill you physically, it will get you emotionally. But its ultimate goal is to kill you spiritually.

The Bible tells us in Ecclesiastes 3:1–9 that there is a time for everything. And I believe that there is a time to get angry at things like child molestation and child neglect and child endangerment and domestic violence. There is a time to war against evil.

We ought to be angry enough to do war in the spirit realm and fight against the works of the devil as spiritual soldiers.

Anger that has the right focus on the right object can accomplish much. A good example is Mothers Against Drunk Drivers (MADD). They were angry enough to go out and raise the awareness of how dangerous it is to drink and drive. And as a result, the laws has changed dramatically for drunk drivers. It is good for us to be angry enough to expose the devil for who he is.

Anger can be a valuable force if we put it to constructive use in our lives and in our families and in our communities.

Jesus became angry when abuse of the temple took place in Mark 11:15–17. It was constructive anger because he purged out the corruption and corrected the abuses he saw there. And the Christ in us should be angry about abuse and exploitation, yet without sin.

Do something constructive and move on. Don't let the devil keep you in bondage. Don't let the devil keep you living in a maze. A maze is when you cannot find peace or harmony in your life because everything is mixed up, bound, and out of order.

When you allow anger and unforgiveness to live in you, you have given the devil a foothold. So many people have given the devil a foothold in their lives because they have nursed and harbored anger and bitterness in their hearts.

When anger and unforgiveness are unresolved, it opens the door to a spirit of anger, and it is demonic. Get rid of stored-up anger and don't allow it to accumulate in the future. If you have unresolved anger and bitterness in your life, you are not right with God. The devil's detours are spiritual, so we must attack in the spiritual realm, not in the carnal realm of anger and unforgiveness. The Bible tells us in 2 Corinthians 10:4, "The weapons of our warfare are not carnal, but are mighty through God to the pulling down of strongholds." Thus this means you are to fight for your marital relationship and your family by walking upright in the Lord, reading the word of God so that your mind can be transformed. As the apostle Paul instructs from the word of God in Romans 12:1, "Be transformed by the renewing of your mind, and we are to humble ourselves and prevail and war in prayer, because it is a spiritual battle." In this spiritual battle, there are three major battlefields that the devil is targeting for destruction: (1) your person, (2) your family, and (3) the church.

He will start with your personal life because if he can rip you off by bringing tragedies against you, he can keep you enslaved. Abuse is one of the things the devil will bring upon you to try to put you in permanent bondage. The devil abuses the abuser and uses the abuser to abuse others. Remember, there is no way to catch a robbing, thieving murderer until we get the identity correct. When you identify the bandit, then you can bind him in the name of Jesus.

Anger causes people to continue abusing each other and ultimately destroy family relationships.

In Ephesians 6:12, Paul tells us, "For we wrestle not against flesh and Blood, but against principalities, against the rulers of darkness of this world, against spiritual wickedness in high places.

You don't have to continue in a state of unrest. Jesus is the only one that can give you rest from unwanted anger. In Matthew 11:28–30, Jesus says, "Come to me, all who are weary and heavy-laden, and I will give you rest. Take my yoke upon you, and learn from me, for I am gentle and humble in heart; and *you shall find rest for your souls.* For my yoke is easy, and my load is light" (NAS). Why carry baggage that you don't have to carry? Jesus wants to carry all your baggage if you will unload it by giving it to Him.

Reflection

1. How can you get relief from all your baggage?

_____

_____

_____

_____

_____

_____

_____

_____

2. In John 10:10, Jesus calls the devil a _____.

   Burglars like to do their business in the dark. When you want to protect your home, you install more lights all around your home. This is the same thing you must do in your spiritual life.

3. To keep the demon of anger and destruction out, we must learn to walk in the light and communicate in our relationships in the light.

What does 1 John 1:7 tell you to do?

_____

_____

_____

_____

_____

_____

_____

_____

Stay in the light by staying very close to the light of the world, and the thief will be exposed when he tries to sneak in to bring in anger and discord through arguments into your marriage and your relationship. Instead, spread a floodlight around your life. Make it hard for the devil to attack. Do this by spending time with Jesus together as a couple or as a family. Give time to prayer and Bible study each day.

What does Psalm 119:11–16 tell you to do, and how can you do this?

_____

_____

_____

_____

_____

_____

_____

_____

_____

CHAPTER 7

Depression Must Go

Much of the dysfunction seen in the relationship between some black men and black women can be credited to depression. Given the background of the black man and the black woman in this society and what they have both had to undergo just to survive, being depressed can be expected. Much of the anger comes from depression. But what they need to remember is that they are supposed to be on the same team, not opposite teams. Team members work together, not against each other. Depression is not new in this world system. Depression is not relegated to the weak. Depression is reported in the Bible as plaguing one of the most important prophets of the Bible, Elijah. There are many Elijahs in the black community that do not know their potential in Christ Jesus because they are depressed, full of fear, and angry; and they take it out on their households and relationships. Depression causes the black man to look like a lazy, non-industrious man. This ends up causing him to feel hopeless and useless. Then he vents upon his spouse and/or family members until they are isolated. Everyone runs away from him because they are afraid and tired of the explosive venting.

Yes, Elijah was a man of God, yet he was depressed too. Depression is a real culprit. I believe that when we look at 1 Kings 19, we can see

Elijah suffering from clinical depression. In this passage of scripture, we find that Elijah was plagued with fear.

- In 1 Kings 19:3, the Bible says, "Elijah was afraid and ran for his life."

- In 1 Kings 19:4, the Bible says, "Elijah said, 'I have had enough, LORD, take my life; I am no better than my ancestors.'"

- In 1 Kings 19:5, the Bible says that "then he lay down under the tree and fell asleep." Depression causes one to feel excessive fatigue and to sleep most of the time. Elijah might have slept for days.

- In 1 King 19:10, Elijah complains about his conditions. He says, "I have been very zealous for the LORD God Almighty. The Israelites have rejected your covenant, broken down your altars, and put your prophets to death with the sword. I am the only one left, and now they are trying to kill me too." And he experienced this depression for a long time, maybe two months.

As it is reported to us in the Holy Scriptures, Elijah had some great encounters with the Lord and he'd had some great successes in his ministry, yet this did not exempt him from depression. God is no respecter of persons. If He healed Elijah of depression, He can heal you too. But you must decide that you will consult God about your depression, your fears, and your entire life.

God did not leave Elijah in depression. And He will not leave you in depression if you trust Him. One of the commonest things some people do is consult their friends first or begin trying to hide behind alcohol and drugs. This is a tragedy. This is exactly where Satan wants you. God is the only one who will never leave you nor forsake you. He will not condemn you. He will not put your business in the streets. He will pick you up, heal, and deliver you. Elijah was down in the dumps, but that's not where God left him. God didn't say, "Well, Elijah, you have a chemical imbalance, and since Zoloft and Xanax and Paxil have not been invented yet, it looks like you just have to keep on suffering."

Long before mental hospitals and mental clinics and psychiatrists and psychologists were invented, God healed a man with depression. He is the same God yesterday, today, and forever. He is the Great Physician.

The Bible tells us that God didn't harass or push him. God just let Elijah sleep. And then God sent His angel to feed and nurture Elijah. Then God sent Elijah on an errand down to the desert for forty days and nights.

God did not give Elijah some long lecture. Notice God just gave Elijah love and rest and a task to show him he was still useful.

As God continued to deal with Elijah's depression, in the right time, God gave Elijah the divine prescription for depression. God sent Elijah to Mount Horeb, the Mount of God where the law was given to Moses. In other words, God sent Elijah to church. The church is the best place to go to deal with depression because it is a spiritual hospital. It is a place where God will speak to you through the shepherd. In 1999 Duke University conducted a study of nearly four thousand older adults. Their findings were that going to church and participating in worship is related to lower rates of depression and anxiety. Prayer, Bible study, and worshipping God are powerful antidepressants.

The best medicine for depression is talking to God about your problems. Elijah talked to God about his problems. And God counseled Elijah and pointed out to him where he was going wrong. God dealt with the false beliefs, the false ideas that were causing Elijah's depression. If you rest in false beliefs, you will give these false beliefs power over you and you can find yourself in bondage. It is best to build your life and relationships on the truth, not on falsehood.

The way in which Elijah responded to God shows us just how he had interpreted information about God wrongly. In 1 Kings 19:14, Elijah replied to God and said, "I have been zealous for the LORD God of hosts: because the children of Israel have forsaken thy covenant, thrown down thine altars, and slain thy prophets with the sword; and I, even I only am left; and they seek my life, to take it away." Elijah seems to be thinking that he has been working hard and God has been just sitting by doing nothing. God goes on to instruct Elijah in 1 Kings 19–15 to go anoint Jehu and Elisha to succeed him as prophet. What looks like a disaster is really a victory. God's plans are perfect. In essence, he was telling Elijah, "I've got it all under control. It may not look like I'm doing anything, but in the end, you will see if you just trust and obey."

Most depressed people don't think God is doing anything. They are very low on hope and confidence. God is hard for them to see at a time of depression. But they need to remember, just like Elijah needed to remember, that God never stops working in our lives. God never sleeps or slumbers. God is not hard of hearing or seeing. God is all powerful. You can rest in him and know that he is looking out for your best interest. But you must trust and obey.

Another well-known man of our time suffered depression, and his name is J. C. Penney. He owned and managed over 1,700 stores during the first part of the twentieth century. And although his business made him very wealthy, when the Great Depression struck the country, it caused him great worry and pain. He said, "I was so harassed with worries that I couldn't sleep and developed an extremely painful ailment." Penney ended up in the Kellogg Sanitarium. Penney reported that "a rigid treatment was prescribed, but nothing helped." He was constantly tormented by periods of hopelessness and despair. He was losing the will to live. Penney reported, "I got weaker and weaker day by day. I was broken and nervous and filled with despair, unable to see even a ray of hope. I had nothing to live for. I felt that I hadn't a friend left in the world, that even my family had turned against me." His doctor gave him a sedative. However, it quickly wore off, and Penney awakened with the conviction that he was living the last night of his life. "Getting out of bed, I wrote farewell letters to my wife and to my son, saying that I did not expect to live to see the dawn." Penney awakened the next morning, surprised to find himself alive. Making his way down the hallway of the hospital, he could hear singing coming from the little chapel where devotional exercises were held each morning. The words of the hymn he heard being sung spoke deeply to him. He went into the chapel and listened to the singing, the reading of the scripture lesson, and the prayer. "Suddenly something happened," he said. "I can't explain it. I can only call it a miracle. I felt as if I had been instantly lifted out of the darkness of a dungeon into a warm, brilliant sunlight. I felt as if I had been transported from hell to paradise. I felt the power of God as I had never felt it before." In a life-transforming moment, Penney knew that God, with His love, was there to help. "From that day to this, my life has been free from worry," he declared. "The most dramatic and glorious 20 minutes of my life were those I spent in that chapel that morning" (http://en.wikipedia.org/wiki/James Cash Penny).

The words from the hymn that ministered to Penney were these:

> Be not dismayed whate'er betide, God will take care of you;
> Beneath His wings of love abide, God will take care of you.
> God will take care of you, through every day, o'er all the
> way; He will take care of you, God will take care of you.

The treatment for depression is not living in anger or isolation or alcohol or drugs. It is simply total surrender to God. It is simply knowing that God will take care of you. God sent Elijah to church for a cure of depression. God sent Penney to church to be healed of depression too. And He is sending you to church to be fed spiritual food. It will nourish you to real life and bring you out of depression too.

Reflection

1. Depression can keep you from experiencing your full potential and ultimately cause you to miss your destiny. You must forgive yourself first and then forgive those who you believe have wronged you and then move on into the blessings that await you.

Read and *commit to memory* Lamentations 3:21–23 and discuss how it helps you.

_____

_____

_____

_____

Read 1 Thessalonians 5:14–16 and state what to practice always.

_____

_____

_____

_____

If you have not already joined a church or are not in regular attendance in a Bible-believing church, do so very soon. Fellowship with the saints. Attend the prayer services and the Bible studies. Make friends with those in your church and become involved with serving as God leads.

Read Ephesians 4:14–18 and discuss what you should do to bring more harmony into your life.

_____

_____

_____

_____

_____

Study Romans 3:23 and Romans 6:23 and commit them to memory.

Read John 1:12 and write it out.

_____

_____

_____

_____

_____

_____

_____

_____

_____

Read 1 John 5:14–15 and meditate on what you should do to be secure.

_____

_____

_____

_____

_____

_____

_____

_____

CHAPTER 8

The Spirit of Jezebel

James E. Blackwell reports in his book, *The Black Community Diversity and Unity*: "Black families vary considerably in the structure of family authority. The authority figure may be either the male or female or both may share authority equally." He further states that a household headed by a male is a patriarchal household, and a household that is headed by a female is a matriarchal household. When both the husband and wife share equally in the responsibilities, it is then classified as an equalitarian household. Many black families have been seen as matriarchal households in the past. However, they are rapidly moving into equalitarian households (Blackwell 1975).

Much of the learned behavior of the black woman to be matriarchal stems from her having been put in that place for such a long time. It began during slavery when black men had to leave their families. Historical and sociological evidence shows that usually they did so under force. If they did not obey the forced order to leave their families, they would be killed instantly.

When organized slavery was over, the damage had already been done to the family structure and was being perpetuated through the lack of viable employment for the black male. The black female was in charge of the household because many times she would be the only one to have an income. This caused division, rebellion, and miscommunication in the relationship between the black man and the black woman. When there is rebellion between a husband and a wife, they are turned against each other, and when they are turned against each other, they are turned against God. And when you are turned against God, you give the devil free access to your affairs, and your home will be filled with chaos. When a woman will not allow a man to take his rightful place in the home, she is operating under the spirit of Jezebel. When a man will not take his rightful place in the home as he is supposed to, he forces his wife to appear to have the Jezebel spirit.

Who Is Jezebel?

The Bible reports Jezebel as the daughter of Ethbaal, the king of the Zidonians, and the wife of Ahab, the king of Israel. This was the first time that a king of Israel had allied himself by marriage with a heathen princess, and the alliance was, in this case, of a peculiarly disastrous kind. Jezebel was not an Israelite. Ahab was no more than a puppet in the hands of Jezebel. He knew what was right and had even seen the power of the real God Jehovah firsthand, but the evil influence of Jezebel controlled him. He was influenced by whatever she said, and he went along with her as she seduced him into believing her lies. Jezebel has engraved her name on history as the representative of those who are crafty, malicious, revengeful, and cruel to the bone. She was so persuasive and controlling. She had 450 prophets ministering under her care to Baal, besides 400 prophets of the groves, who ate at her table. She was highly idolatrous and debased. Jezebel sought to lead the country away into idolatry. This type of thinking is rebellious and will not accept any kind of authority or orders. This is the kind of spirit that will not accept anyone telling it that it is doing wrong. Jezebel hated Elijah and was angry and embittered at the fate that had befallen her priests of Baal at Mt. Carmel. She made a vow to kill Elijah and to shut him up once and for all. Jezebel hated the move of God then and now. The spirit of Jezebel can work in all kinds of people that have a negative/carnal attitude.

The Jezebel spirit hates God's order, God's plans, and God's activities. A person that is allowing the spirit of Jezebel to rule will always be opposed to listening to advice given by anyone else and will always go against wise counsel, because the spirit of Jezebel is a selfish spirit that has a me-myself-and-I attitude. Anyone allowing that spirit to rest on them will not and cannot understand the things of God. This is the kind of person that will argue you down about things that he or she is wrong about because he or she has to be right about everything.

- The Jezebel spirit is the spirit of the devil.
- It hates correction.
- It is manipulative.
- It is controlling.
- It is rebellious.
- It is intimidating and seducing.

We can see the spirit of Jezebel working in Herodia because she hated John the Baptist. In Mark 6:18 the Bible tells us that John tried to give her wise counsel and she rejected it. Verse 18, "Because John had said to Herod, 'It is not lawful for you to have your brother's wife.'" Therefore, Herodias held it against him and wanted to kill him, but she could not. For Herod feared John, knowing that he was a just and holy man, and he protected him.

Herod was willing to protect John the Baptist until the spirit of Jezebel came in and seduced him, and at this point he began to obey the evil spirit of Jezebel. Mark 6:22 tells us, "And when Herodias' daughter herself came in and danced, and pleased Herod and those who sat with him, the king said to the girl, 'Ask me whatever you want, and I will give it to you.'"

This is a captivating, manipulative spirit that will overwhelm those that it is targeting if they allow themselves to become entangled with it. That is exactly what happen to Herod. He was tricked by the spirit of Jezebel, and he granted her request.

The spirit of Jezebel is deceptive. This is the same spirit that came against Jesus in the form of Judas; however, Jesus was not deceived by Judas because He was God. As you rely on Jesus, you will not be deceived by the Jezebel spirit either. The Jezebel spirit will use anyone that it can in an effort to destroy God's plans and purposes.

Marriage is God's plan, and Jezebel hates all God's plans. Thus, the Jezebel spirit will slip into your marriage and try to destroy it. But you must be aware of what to look for and how to avoid the pitfalls of such a destructive spirit. The greatest pitfall is the fall of acting out of God's order for the marriage. When you take a position in the marriage that you have not been ordained by God to take, you open the door for demonic control.

Some women did not start off with a Jezebel spirit, but they allowed themselves to be pushed into it by a frightened man who would not take the leadership role that God had given him. But you need to know that this is a trick of the enemy to get you in a position to be destroyed like Jezebel was in 2 Kings 9:34–37.

There are many black men that have acquired a low self-esteem because of the societal pressures he has found himself in. These are men who cannot get on the right track when it comes to being consistently employed. When a man cannot be the breadwinner in his house, he may feel less than a man and may begin to act less than a man.

Some men may begin to act like a boy rather than the man of the house. And this is when conflict and confusion begin to take over his household. Sometimes when this happens, a spirit of Jezebel will take charge of the woman of the house. If she gets comfortable with the spirit of Jezebel, she may begin to rule everything, and if her husband give her some feedback, she may no longer receive it. At this point he may hear something like this, "You don't tell me what to do. I make more money than you, and I will do what I think is best." If she is planning to continue in the marriage, she should be trying to motivate him to do better by being more positive in her behavior. After all, since slavery to now the black man has been the last hired and the first fired. He needs someone to empathize with him and help direct him to those things that will help him, such as going back to school to acquire a higher education or motivate and work with him to launch his own business. Functioning in the spirit of Jezebel will not benefit the woman nor the man. If you begin to allow the Jezebel spirit to hang around, it will take over you with the intentions to destroy your marriage. The devil is a greedy, selfish, unloving spirit that comes to kill you and your family. Your children will model what they see you do because you are their role model.

It is dangerous to live with someone with whom you must use accusations such as the ones listed below. These are the kind of accusations that come from a Jezebel spirit:

- When are you going to grow up.
- I make more money. You don't tell me what to do.
- If it wasn't for me, you wouldn't be anything.
- This is my house, and I will put you out anytime I want to.
- And if you don't go, I will call the police on you.

It would be better to separate and seek professional counseling before you come to something such as the above.

The Story about Lucy

This reminds me of a lady who allowed the Jezebel spirit to ruin her life and her daughter's life. Lucy had no respect for men at all. The Jezebel spirit was on a mission to kill her, and she did not recognize it. The spirit of Jezebel had taken the front seat in her life. She was so selfish that if her husband did not bring every dime of his check home, she would throw a fit. He couldn't even buy a hamburger out of his paycheck. He was just like a prisoner in this marriage. And she thought having sex with her husband was enough reason for him to bow down and give her anything she wanted.

One day, Jack, Lucy's husband, kept a few dollars of his paycheck and she was upset about it. They had argued about it for hours. Lucy thought he had given the money to another woman. Jack, tired of defending himself and explaining the fact that he was tired of being without any money in his pocket, got up and took a walk down to the corner store. While he was at the cash register paying for his goods, he heard a loud voice screaming profanity and insults. He looked around, and there was Lucy, with a gun that he did not know she had. He turned to run, and as he ran out of the store and down the street, she shot him down in the streets.

She had not learned how to give love or receive love. She had not grown up in a loving environment. She would talk about her unloving childhood often as if she was in mourning.

Don't Get Stuck Mourning over the Past

Every one of us has things in our past that we would like to go back and change. But this is impossible, and since we cannot change the past, we must let go of the past and live in the present. What happened in the past can be sweet or bitter, but it cannot be changed. The best thing we can do is learn to start fresh with God each new morning. Seize the opportunity to do good and to enjoy life as we have it right now. Don't allow the past to rob you of the enjoyment and sweetness and peace of the present as you grow older. Trust God each day for His blessings and help for that day because he is the same God past, present, and future. We have to Move on to grow.

Prayer

Father God, I repent for trying to make things happen my way. Forgive me for manipulating and controlling others. Forgive me for thinking I know better than You about what is good for my life. Jesus, come into my heart and be my Lord and Savior. Help me to learn to have a hands-off attitude. Help me to trust You with the plans and purpose You have for me and for my loved ones. I bind the Jezebel spirit, renouncing this spirit and commanding it to go in the name of Jesus. I reject all Jezebel suggestions of selfish ambition for myself, my child, my spouse, my parents, or anyone close to me.

Forgive me for trying to put other people into bondage with my desires, or even words I may have spoken against them when they didn't choose my way. Father God, in the name of Jesus, please help me, by the power of the Holy Spirit, to live this out each day of my life. I humbly ask You to remind me whenever I fall back into that old pattern. Keep me on the straight and narrow path to holiness so that I can walk in Your will and Your way. In Jesus's name I pray. Amen.

Reflection

Isaiah 46:4 tells us that He is the God that has _____ you.

He is the God that made you and will _____ you.

He is the God that will sustain and will _____ you.

In Philippians 3:13, Paul tells us, "No, dear brothers and sisters, I am still not all I should be, but I am focusing all my energies on this one thing: forgetting the past and looking forward to what lies."

"Regrets are like a dirty window that keeps us from seeing clearly what is in front of us. But God is in the cleaning business. He washes away the sins of the past as well as the guilt over those sins. If he forgets them completely, so can you" (*TouchPoints for Women* 1996).

A humble spirit erases a Jezebel spirit: Ezekiel 18:31 tells us, "Put all your rebellion behind you, and get for yourselves a new heart and a new spirit." Thus, God says stop.

Ezekiel 36:26 tells us, "I will give you a new heart with new and right desires, and I will put a new spirit in you. I will take out your stony heart of sin and give you a new, obedient heart."

Let go and let God give you a new heart in harmony with him today!

CHAPTER 9

Samson and the Flesh

Judges chapter 13 begins the story of the life of Samson. The Israelites served the Lord for twenty-five years, but as soon as the children grew up, they wanted to be copycats and worship other gods just like their heathen neighbors did. So, they made images and placed them in their cities and under the trees in their yards, and there, they worshipped them. Because of their idol worship, trouble came to them. The strong, cruel Philistines were their troublemakers. The Israelites that lived near the Philistines found themselves under the rule of the Philistines for forty years. Dagon was the Philistines' god. Dagon had the face and hands of a man but the body of a fish. This evil ugly thing had a temple built to it by the Philistines.

Manoah and his wife were Israelites that served the Lord. Manoah's wife was barren, yet God gave them a child miraculously because He was going to use this child (Samson) to deliver Israel from the Philistines. God gave them strict instructions that Samson was to never cut his hair or drink wine because he belonged to God. This was called a Nazarite vow.

Samson disobeyed God and followed after the flesh, and it cost him his life in the end. The enemy of our souls has a battle plan that is very similar. The scripture tells us that the road that leads to destruction is broad, and I believe there are warning signs all the way down the road saying, "*don't turn on to that pathway because there is destruction!*" Yet many ignore the signs and keep on going because it feels good to them. God will give you instructions, but He will not violate your will and force you to obey. You must do this yourself.

According to T. Austin-Sparks, "As an instrument the soul has to be won, mastered and ruled in relation to the higher and different ways of God. It is spoken of so frequently in the Scriptures as being something over which we must gain and exercise authority. Psalm 62:5 says, 'My soul, wait thou only upon God; for my expectation is from Him'" (Watchman Nee 1965).

A carnal man will choose everything according to his own selfish reason. Usually, he chooses to go into a relationship for purely carnal reasons, deciding to get involved in a courtship or get married to a woman because she has a job, or because she is physically built a certain way, or because she is of a certain complexion, etc. These are all carnal reasons. The reason for building a relationship with a person should never be solely based on these external things; a carnal man will be more concerned with these things than the real person with which he is getting involved. Looks should be secondary to what is in the heart of a person.

Get attracted to the deeper side of the woman before you get so hung up on the outer side of the woman. If you do not take these things into account, you will have a miserable marriage (Judg. 16:1, 4–5, 18–20).

There was misery after marriage for Samson. Whether or not Samson knew what love was in the first place, he appears to have lost the meaning of love here. The Scriptures points to the fact that Samson's wife did not love him either, because she tricked him into telling her the riddle just so she could give it to those who demanded it. He had so little respect for her he called her a heifer to other men. In Judges 14:18c, "Samson said, 'if ye had not plowed with my heifer, ye had not found out my riddle.'" Because Samson did not choose a wife in a godly way, he ended up marrying what he called a heifer. He married a woman out of lust, and when the marriage flopped, he gave up on marriage completely and satisfied himself in other ways—namely, he became a womanizer. He turned to the harlot. He abandoned the sanctified ordinance of marriage that was established by God. Samson's own solution was to pursue the lust of the flesh. Samson became a slave to sin. He was disobedient to God, which was sin, and we can see that one sin leads to another sin. He ended up leaving the harlot to take up with another woman in what he again called a love affair. But he did not really love Delilah either, because he was still driven by the flesh. And because he was so driven by the flesh, he never knew what true love was. He failed in this so-called relationship also, because he once again failed to look for the beauty within the woman before looking at the beauty on the outside of the woman. In the Hebrew, the name Delilah (*Dalal*) means "to slacken, bring low, be emptied, and to fail." And because Samson went for the lust of the flesh and pursued sin, his relationship with God was weakened. Samson was lowered so much by sin, the Bible says, "He did not know that the LORD had departed from him" (Judg. 16:20c, NASB). Delilah's very name was symbolic of Samson's self-destruction and sinful life. Delilah virtually caused Samson to lose his life simply because she was the wrong woman for him. Samson lost his life because he chose to run from woman to woman as a womanizer does.

There are many black men (not all) who have chosen to become a womanizer too, running from woman to woman, leaving women with babies and adding to the absentee-father list, children with single-mom homes left to fend for themselves. This is just irresponsible, and it is your fault that your child is out in a street gang looking for love in all the wrong places. Don't look to society to deliver you and your children. Look to God to deliver you and your children. He can and He will if you will submit and surrender to God, the one that cares about you. Seek Him for guidance.

- It is best to let God lead, guide, and direct you to that family woman to raise a family.
- It is best to educate yourself and use the talents God gave you.
- Love is not sex.
- Love is not a physical attraction.
- Love is not romance.

It is destructive to make the same mistake repeatedly as Samson did. He continued his lust until he was trapped by a death trap named Delilah. He was killed before he could finish the work he was blessed by God to do in the first place. What a waste. You cannot conquer life by running from woman to woman as soon as the boat gets a little rocky. That is the way of a loser. You conquer life to the extent that you have a relationship with God. Samson's power was because he had a covenant with God. He had power because the

Lord was upon him. But Samson, the carnal man, did not finish his job of delivering Israel from the Philistine oppression; that was done under the prophet Samuel and King David. We can only wonder what Samson could have accomplished if he had followed his calling 100 percent. Samson had a responsibility to deliver the Israelites, but he paid more attention to his flesh and evaded his responsibility, so God had to get someone else to take Samson's responsibility to get the job done. You cannot do anything of good without Jesus Christ as Lord and Savior of your life.

Prayer

Father God, in the name of Jesus, I thank you for sending Jesus to die on the cross for my sins, to be buried, and to rise again on the third day. I confess all my sins, and I repent now, and I turn my life over to you. I cannot do this any longer myself. I have tried to handle it my way, and I have failed. Deliver me from myself, take my life, and make me what you want me to be. Jesus, come into my life and dwell in me that I may live through you. Save me! Help me! Lead me, guide and direct me, and give me the mind of Christ and fill me with your precious Holy Spirit. In Jesus's name I pray. Amen.

Reflection

1. Second Corinthians 6:14–17 says, "Be ye not unequally yoked together with unbelievers: for what fellowship hath righteousness with unrighteousness? And what communion hath light with darkness? And what communion hath Christ with Belial? Or

what part hath he that believeth with and infidel? And what agreement hath the temple of God with idols? For ye are the temple of the living God; as God hath said, I will dwell in them, and walk in them; and I will be their God, and they shall be my people. Therefore come out from them and be separate, says the Lord. Touch no unclean thing, and I will receive you." (KJV)

(Maybe it would be a good idea to make an appointment with your local pastor for further consultation.)

1. Study Judges 13:1–5: Samson was from birth.
2. Samuel was not supposed to intermingle with the _____, because they were.
3. In Judges 14:5, Samson disobeyed God when he _____.
4. In Judges 14:3, Samson parents' counsel.

- Do not lose God's power through carelessness.
- The Holy Spirit is here to restore power to your life if you will obey the commandments of God, walk with a pure heart in his sight, and do not rest until you have recovered all your lost ground.

CHAPTER 10

The Responsibility of a Father

All fathers have been charged with the responsibility to teach, train, love, and raise their children according to the word of God. When a father successful raise his children they have a higher chance of avoiding being raised by the street gangs and the prison system.

According to the fact sheet on black disparities in youth incarceration, "forty two percent of youths in placement are black, even though Black Americans comprise only 15% of all youth across the United States".(The Sentencing Project By Joshua Rovner, 2023) This is the responsibility of the father as well as the mother's, yet it can be difficult to raise children today because youth value other peers opinion very much. As a result, families could benefit by lovingly consistently teaching their family values to their children by modeling as well as explaining why these are your family values. Also, your family values may be more acceptably received if you listen to your child's fears, concerns and opinions.

The Bible says in Ephesians 6:4, "And Ye Fathers, provoke not your children to wrath: but bring them up in the nurture and admonition of the Lord." How are you going to do that if you don't know how to train a child? You may be saying, "I did not have a daddy nor a positive male role model myself, and I don't know the first thing about raising a child."

The answer is a relationship with the Lord God. Stay before the Lord in prayer. Seek wise counsel from a trusted and respectable pastor or counselor. Stay in the word of God, and as you seek the Lord for directions, He will help you in all that you do in raising your children.

In Colossians 3:21 Paul warns us that if we proceed to provoking our children, we take a chance in causing them embitterment and discouragement. The Bible is the best guide you could ever use to raise your children. As the word says, do not embitter your children. This is sometimes done by calling children demeaning names. Emotional and physical abuse is neglectful, careless and damaging to children. If the only attention you give your child is negative attention, the bonding process could possibly become defective. The only way that your child will be able to communicate is in a negative way. He or she may fight with his or her other sisters and brothers or other people to communicate. And if all that child sees his or her parents do is communicate negatively, that behavior will be acted out in that child's life and as a result, that behavior or child rearing pattern may be passed down for generations. A father should take the responsibility to protect and nurture his children so they can feel like their home is a safe and loving environment. They should grow up knowing they can depend on the head of the household to make their house a home.

It is irresponsible to discipline your child by labeling your child as a troublemaker or evil or saying things like "you are bound to turn out bad." A child who has been the recipient of this kind of talk may begin to act accordingly. Sociologically speaking, this is known as a self-fulfilling prophecy. But more importantly, biblically speaking, this is called cursing with your tongue. James 3:9–10 tells us, "With it we bless our God and Father; and with it we curse men, who have been made in the similitude of God; out of the same mouth proceed both blessing and cursing. My brethren, these things ought not to be" (NKJV). As a father, you should always be speaking blessings into your child's life. Build up your child with words of affirmation. And even when you discipline or punish your child, it should be done in love. Always guard your words because words are powerful. Proverbs 18:21 tells us, "Death and life are in the power of the tongue, and those who love it will eat its fruit" (NKJV). Whatever you speak into your child's life is like a seed planted, and it will yield fruit. The kind of fruit depends on what has been spoken into that child's life.

Irresponsible fathers, unloving fathers, and absentee fathers contribute a lot to juvenile delinquency. Most of those who become delinquents are those that do not identify with positive role models. Children need positive role models. Children coming out of a loveless home may reflect close ties to friends and people outside of the family home. One study by Bandura and Walters (1958), for example, noted that "antisocial boys experience a lack of paternal affection as well as parental rejection, which prevent identification with parental standards and values." Another report by Allen and Sandhu (1967) states, "institutionalized delinquents and 178 nondelinquents disclosed that low family affection and increased hostility toward the parents are factors leading to the possibility of their children joining violent gangs" (Horton and Hunt 1972).

First Thessalonians 2:11–12 tells us, "As ye know how we exhorted and comforted and charge every one of you, as a father doth his children, that ye would walk worthy of God, who hath called you unto his kingdom and glory." A father should encourage his child and not say things that make his child feel like a failure.

This should be on the top of the list in being honorable. Men of honor have the following character traits:

- They are men of integrity and moral soundness.
- They are men of honesty and uprightness.
- They are spiritual leaders.
- These are men that will lead their families to Christ.
- These are men that seek to be more like Jesus every day.
- They have right standing with God.
- This means they are excellent role models.

Fathers need to be their children's best teachers in life and in spiritual truths. If you don't teach your child, the world will.

Being a father is most important. I believe that it makes it difficult for a child to see God as a good father if his relationship with his natural father is one of neglect, abandonment, and abuse. A father that portrays indifference and disinterest all the time can make it hard for his child to look to God. An honorable father will not lead his child away from salvation, but he will lead his child to salvation. He will learn spiritual truths through the Holy Scriptures and teach them to his children, because it is the only source that has all the answers to our lives. It is the responsibility of the father to make sure that he prepares his children to die as well as to live. Prepare them to make it into the kingdom of God. Prepare them for eternal life in heaven with God. The choice is yours. Be a beacon of light in this dark and dying world to your child. But you must be born again yourself and know and love God yourself before you can lead your child to Christ. You cannot lead anyone where you are not going yourself. Jesus said, "I am the resurrection and the life; sayeth the Lord. He that believeth in Me, though he were dead, yet shall he live. And whosoever liveth and believeth in Me shall never die" (John 11:25–26a). Anyone who loves his child does not want to see his child in hell.

Reflection

1. Read Hebrews 12:7–14: According to this text, what will a good and loving parent do with his or her child?

_____

_____

_____

_____

_____

_____

_____

2. What will discipline produce?

_____

_____

3. If you are not disciplining, you are _____ children.

4. Read Deuteronomy 6:4–8. According to this text, what are we to do with the commandments?

_____

_____

_____

_____

_____

_____

_____

_____

_____

CHAPTER 11

Giants Are Subdued by the Lord

There is no doubt that the plight of the black man and the black woman in this society has been in the past and is in the present still a giant problem that can only be subdued by the Lord.

- There is the battle of finding employment that will pay enough money to pay the bills.
- There is the battle of finding affordable housing in a neighborhood that is not drug infested or crime infested.
- There is the battle of being able to provide proper education for their children.
- There is still the battle of discrimination in many areas of the black man's and the black woman's lives, which in turn bring on the giants of worry, doubt, fear, anxiety, depression, and insecurity to a very large degree.
- The common giants of drugs in our schools and our communities, gang warfare in the communities, and drive-by shootings are battles that we need the Lord to intervene on.

These giants come to discourage you and to take you out. They come to make you think that you are of no worth on this earth. And if you pay attention to them, you will give up on everything because everywhere you look there is a giant. But the truth of the matter is that you can be a winner if you allow the Lord to fight your battle. Don't give up on your family. Fight for your family by dwelling in unity and not division. Psalm 133:1 says, "Behold, how good and how pleasant it is for brethren to dwell together in unity!" And verse 3 says that if you dwell in unity, blessings will come upon you. "For there the LORD commanded the blessing—life for forevermore."

In 1 Samuel 17: 45–46a, the Bible tells us, "Then said David to the Philistine, thou comest to me with a sword, and with a spear, and with a shield: but I come to thee in the name of the LORD of hosts, the God of the armies of Israel, whom thou hast defied. This day will the LORD deliver thee into mine hand."

The bottom line is that we have a choice, and we are faced with deciding who are we relying on to defeat our giants? Who are we depending on to carry our burdens?

If you depend on those who enslaved you and used you for their benefit to carry your burdens, you are then empowering your giants. God wants you to have complete dependence on Him and Him alone. He is the only one who will and can deliver you from your giants.

In 1 Samuel 17:41–44, the Bible tells us,

> And the Philistine came on and drew near unto David; and the man that bare the shield went before him. And when the Philistine looked about, and saw David, he

disdained him: for he was but a youth, and ruddy, and of a fair countenance. And the Philistine said unto David, "Am I a dog, that thou comest to me with staves?" and the Philistine cursed David by his gods. And the Philistine said to David, "Come to me, and I will give thy flesh unto the fowls of the air and to the beast of the field."

Goliath defeated himself when he cursed David. The word translated as *cursed* is the same word used in Genesis 12:3a, "And I will bless them that bless thee, and curse him that curseth thee." Goliath messed up right here when he cursed David, and since David was one of God's people, God had an obligation by His covenant to curse Goliath.

God could have killed Goliath before David fought Goliath, but he didn't because he wanted to show them all His mighty power in their weakness. Sometimes God will not move our mountains, our giants, but he will give us the strength to climb them first, then take them down.

God cannot lie. Any giant that comes against you will be taken down if you go in the strength of the Lord.

It doesn't matter how big the problem/giant is; with God, it is nothing if you rely on Him. You must walk upright as a mighty man of valor in the Lord, knowing that the battle is not yours, but it is the Lord's.

Goliath was a huge giant, yet nothing to God. The Bible tells us in 1 Samuel 17:4–7, "And there went out a champion out of the camp of the Philistines, named Goliath, of Gath, whose height was six cubits and a span. And he had a helmet of brass upon his head, and he was armed with a coat of mail; and the weight of the coat was five thousand shekels of brass. And he had a greaves of brass upon his legs, and a target of brass between his shoulders. And the staff of his spear was like a weaver's beam; and his spear's head weighed six hundred shekels of iron: and one bearing a shield went before him."

Goliath was a giant with mighty physical strength, and he was a trained warrior with powerful armor. And on the other hand, David was only a five-foot-tall skinny youth and a shepherd boy who had never been in battle before. It was very unbelievable to everyone that David would defeat Goliath.

The black man and the black woman may face challenges in their relationship, many of which stem from poverty and discrimination. These giants can spill over into how they communicate with each other based on the depression and the anxiety that come with the giant problems. And when they begin to look at the giants and then begin to blame each other instead of going to God together in mutual prayer and dependency on God, Goliath can take them and their children over. When you face giant challenges that appear to be overwhelming, remember that you are no match against such great odds but that the battle is the Lord's.

Remember the victory of David over Goliath and be inspired to face your giants with confidence that the Lord will bring victory out of each battle. And always remember: the greater the battle, the greater the victory.

Goliath was David's giant to overcome. It was his distraction and his problem. Goliath was also Israel's giant to overcome. Saul was leading the Israelite army in battle, and the Spirit of the LORD had left him. When the Spirit of the LORD is not present, there will be no faith or confidence in God's leadership. And every day, they woke up and wasted time shaking in their boots to face their giant. It was a waste of time because they did not have the Lord on their side. Their leader did not have the spirit of the Lord.

The only way to defeat the giants of life is to surrender all to God. David knew that he was absolutely nothing without God. He knew that everything he was and everything he had belonged to God. He knew that he had nothing to lose. Even as he stood to go into battle with Goliath, he knew he was there under the power and authority of God. He did not have some hidden agenda to impress Saul and all those around him. David knew that God was bigger than any giant.

My brothers and sisters, there is a lesson to be learned from David. He purposed in his mind that he would bless and praise the Lord at all times. This meant that he would not give up on God when the going got rough, but that he would remember where God brought him from.

In 1 Samuel 17:37, the Bible says, "David said moreover, The LORD that delivered me out of the paw of the lion, and out of the paw of the bear, he will deliver me out of the hand of this Philistine. And Saul said unto David, Go, and the LORD be with thee."

David did not get amnesia about what God had done for him in the past. He knew what God had brought him from. And he knew God was the same God yesterday, today, and forever. He had experienced God coming to his rescue in situations that looked hopeless.

Brothers and sisters, don't get so hung up on the present giant that you forget the even bigger giant that God brought you out of, namely, organized slavery. Look back at how God brought you out of the most notorious form of slavery known to humankind. You are still surviving segregation and racial profiling and many other giants, and you are not annihilated yet. Thank God for His faithfulness.

Just like Goliath put the Israelites in fear, Satan will try to put you in fear and doubt too. Satan was a giant that thought he had Jesus where he wanted him too. Jesus won the battle for you too when he died on that old, rugged cross and was buried in that borrowed tomb and rose on the third day. The battle is won by Jesus. Do you know Him? Is He your Savior? If He is, victory is yours! *Reflection*

1. Read 1 Samuel 17:45–50.

   David stated four times his trust in the Lord before, during, and after the battle. He defeated the giant by following the directions of God. He used the most unlikely things to defeat the giant, and the giant was defeated.

   David told the giant that he came in the_____.

   This means David _____ the Lord to fight his battle as he obeyed the direction of the Lord.

   David had a _____ commitment to God.

2. Read verse 51:

   When you cut off the head of Satan and his imps and demons through spiritual warfare, it will fill their camp with fear and terror. Cut off the head of anger in your household, discord, confusion, and all sin; and you will be cutting off the head of the leading giant in your life. This is how you take the enemy's weapons away from him. Daily, you should remember how God delivered you and to God give the glory.

3. Read Ephesians 6:10–18.

   What is the Christians' armor?

   _____

   _____

   _____

   _____

   _____

   _____

4. Read Deuteronomy 6:4–9 and discuss.

   _____

   _____

   _____

   _____

   _____

   _____

5. Read 2 Timothy 1:5–7. Faith subdues the giant of fear or timidity.

   - Timothy was reminded of the _____ of his mother and grandmother.
   - His mother and grandmother were the only two Christians in his family.

6. Read Genesis 41:41–45.

   Joseph had a _____ record.

   - Joseph survived the giant of jealous and hateful siblings.

7. Slavery versus freedom: Read Romans 13:12–14.

    The Bible tells us to put away the works of darkness and put on the _____ of light. Clothe yourselves with the

_____

    And do not think about how to gratify the desires of the

_____

    To continue living in sin is habit forming and slavery. It is a bondage that can be depressing for those who want to be free in Christ Jesus.

    "God created Adam and Eve to live dependently on Him" (Anderson and Zuehlke 2000). "All temptation is an attempt to get us to live our lives independently of God." This boils down to selfish pride, and selfish pride is "an independent spirit that wants to exalt itself."

    James 4:6 says, "God opposes the proud but gives grace to the humble." Proverbs 16:18 says, "Pride goes before destruction, a haughty spirit before a fall."

    Arrogance, prideful egotism, and unforgiveness set us up for a fall. Never be so prideful that you can't forgive, because unforgiveness is slavery.

CHAPTER 12

How to Love God's Way

In order for the black man and the black woman to redeem their relationship, they need to follow the advice given in 1 Corinthians 13:1–13. The text tells us exactly how to love God's way. Loving God's way means loving with agape love. There needs to be one-to one quality time spent together to promote healing, restoration, and growth in their love relationship.

But getting saved is the first requirement to loving God's way. If you are not saved, it is impossible for you to have agape love in your heart for anyone. That is one reason a saved person should never seek to marry an unsaved person, because that unsaved person cannot and does not love you unconditionally. There is a difference between being in love and being in lust. Lust always has a condition attached to it.

- Lust is selfish.
- Lust is full envy.
- Lust is jealous.
- Lust is temporary.

Everything about lust is connected to pleasing the flesh. It has nothing to do with the heart. But true love is eternal because God is love. The only way that you and I can love God's way is if we are walking with the Lord. Walking with the Lord means that we have surrendered our lives to the Lord. We are under His Lordship and leadership, and we are to follow His example of love. Christ was single-minded in His mission of love "as he spent time with the disciples and communicated with them, teaching them about forgiveness" (Wright 2005).

Love Explained in the Greek

1. Eros Love: This is that sexual and sensual love, that romantic love that causes one to give more attention to the physical feelings of desire. That kind of love that puts butterflies in your stomach and makes your heart skip a beat. This is a component of love that should be in a marriage. There should be a time when a couple can come together and cuddle, pet, and speak softly and sweetly to each other. However, this is not the kind of love that Paul is pointing to in Ephesians 5:23–33, because romantic love is unstable. It is unstable because it is based on feelings and circumstances, and both of you may not be on the same page of feelings all the time. One may be tired and overwhelmed with the bombardment of everyday life, whereas the other may be rested and ready. Thus, there is unreliability in this kind of love because it comes with a condition attached to it.

2. Phileos Love: This word comes from the word "Philadelphia." This is the kind of love that involves friendship. And husband and wife should be friends also. But this also is not the kind of love

that Paul is pointing to. This is the type of love that comes with a condition attached to it too. For example, friends may fall out with each other over trivial things. So-called friends may decide to change addresses, telephone numbers, or attitudes, depending on their needs getting met.

3. Storge Love: This love is the love felt in primary and extended family ties. This is the type of love felt between siblings, uncles, aunts, cousins, etc., some of which you wish you had never known or seen in your life because of the way they act and the way they treat you. But you feel an obligation because of kinship, thus, you continue to associate with them. This kind of love should be in marriages too; however, if it is the only kind of love alive in a marriage, when the children grow up and leave home and the majority of storge love is gone, you may go too because you don't have the type of love needed for the relationship to last. Storge love is the type of love that may be prevailing when the husband stays in the marriage only because of obligatory feelings. Storge love is necessary in all marriages; however, this love comes with a condition too. The condition of family is attached to this type of love. This is not the type of love that Paul is pointing to either.

4. Agape Love: This is a love that rises above the little petty things and sees what is actually necessary. This love looks at the heart and sees the needs of the person. It is the kind of love that can love God's way. The only way the husband and the wife can truly love is to love God's way: unconditional love. God loved us when we were still dead in our sins. The only way to truly love is to give. The Bible tells us in John 3:16, "For God so loved the world, that

he gave his only begotten son that, whosoever believeth in him shall not perish but have everlasting life." God demonstrated his love as sacrifice.

Husbands, Love as God Has Instructed

Ephesians 5:25 tells us, "Husbands, love your wives, just as Christ also loved the Church and gave himself up for her." God is shouting loudly very clear instructions for the way a man is to love a woman. He is saying that if you don't know Jesus Christ personally, you cannot know how to love your wife. How are you going to love your wife as Christ loved the church if you don't even know Him? If a man doesn't love Christ, his whole household will be out of order, because he is ordained to be the leader. A leader disconnected from the only one who can provide everything that is needed to bring sanctification to the home will have a home in chaos. This means the husband should have a sacrificial love for his wife. In other words, he must be ready to give himself because Christ gave Himself for the church. Husbands are the only ones instructed to love sacrificially. Husbands, you cannot give unless you are ready to surrender. Never marry a man that is not willing to give his all for you, even his life. If he is not willing to spend some money on you, if he is not willing to give you his time, if he is not willing to give up others for you, he is not falling in the category of loving you as Christ loves the church, and because of this, he is not worthy of you.

There are many black men who have bought into the idea that society is not going to be fair to them in the employment area, so they give up on being the leader of their households. This has brought about a rift in the relationship of some black man and black woman. Many begin to allow their wives to take care of them. Adam was instructed to be the provider. This doesn't mean that the woman cannot work at all, but it does mean that she is not expected to be responsible for being the head leader of providing for the household. It is not God's will for women to be the sole providers for men. When Satan persuaded Eve to reverse roles and provide the grocery for Adam, they came under a curse and destruction set in. We must operate in God's plans not our own. Proverbs 3:5–6 tells us, "Trust in the LORD with all thine heart; and lean not unto thine own understanding. In all thy ways acknowledge him, and he shall direct thy paths."

A massive number of black men have been incarcerated, and some have become institutionalized. The only way to come out of that state of mind is by the word of God and by obeying God's word and doing it. There is a job for you. There is a seat in the college classroom for you. There is a business for you, but you must believe that God is able to restore you. You must get up off the couch and go and pray as you go preparing yourself to be the leader of your household, then trust God to bring about the plan He has for your life. You must get up and go. You don't have to get caught up in crime.

How Can a Woman Submit?

Paul tells us in Ephesians 5:22–24, "Wives, submit yourselves unto your own husbands, as unto the Lord. For the husband is the head of the wife, even as Christ is the head of the church: and is the savior of the body. Therefore, as the church is subject unto Christ, so let the wives be to their own husbands in everything."

This is a subject that has been misunderstood. It is time to clear up the confusion about women submitting to their husbands. I believe the Bible clearly teaches us that women are to submit to their husbands as their husbands submit to the Lord. Husbands must set an example of submission by being transparent in their submission to the Lord. When they do this, their wives will submit to them. If the wife God gave you sees you submit, respect, love, trust, and obey God, she will submit to you. Submission and love go hand in hand. When you submit to godly leadership, you will then receive the sacrificial love as Christ loved the church. God's order is perfect and without defect.

If you are allowing Jesus Christ as Lord and Savior to rest, rule, and reign in your life, as a result, lying, stealing, cheating, gambling, whore mongering, and disrespecting your wife will not ever be done to her by you. If you love the wife that God gave you, you will not verbally beat her up, you will not physically beat her up, you will not emotionally or mentally abuse and neglect and mistreat her.

If you are supposed to love your wife like Christ love the church, you will not cuss her out and call her all kinds of ugly names, because that is not what Christ would do for the church. The only way to redeem the relationship between some black men and the black women is to fall deeply in love with Christ Jesus. The Bible is a love story to you, telling you how much God loves you so that in the same way, you can love your wife as Christ loves the church.

God's love can be demonstrated in patience and kindness and unselfishness, trusting and persevering. God's love is a lifestyle, not simply a momentary act or a moment's feeling. It is not simply lust.

It is not about good feelings. God's love is a way of life that depicts Christ in us. Christ's love tenderizes us when we walk by the Spirit. He takes out all the toughness and bitterness and selfishness in our hearts toward others who may have mistreated us.

What a wonderful life when Christ lives through us as we yield to Him: a life characterized by His love, His joy, His peace, His patience, and His kindness toward others, only God can bring about these attributes in us.

It is amazing how some people who are mean-spirited, arrogant, opinionated, and even obnoxious are disarmed when God's love in you says words to them that bring healing and restoration. God's love in us is inwardly effective, but it is also outwardly sufficient to help those who treat us wrongly.

Are you loving God's way? When God's people walk by the Spirit, they are always looking out for the needs of others instead of themselves. Internally, they rejoice with the knowledge that God is in control. Externally, they realize that people may not always be nice, but that they are charged to love them with the love of Christ anyway. When God tenderizes your heart, people are softened and disarmed just by your presence. Jesus says in Matthew 11:28–30, "Come unto me, all ye that labor and are heavy laden, And I will give you rest. Take my yoke upon you and learn of me; for I am meek and lowly in heart: and ye shall find rest unto your souls. For my yoke is easy, and my burden is light." Our Lord's commandments are not burdensome to the one who is seeking to live under His Lordship. First John 5:3 tells us, "For this is the love of God, that we keep his commandments: and his commandments are not grievous."

Are You Experiencing God's Love in Your Life?

All you must do is say yes to Christ Jesus and to His will, and He will release His love in you. And it will be a love that no one can deny.

The greatest demonstration of agape love was at the cross of Jesus Christ. At the heart of this kind of love is sacrifice, and this same kind of love is produced in the lives of believers by the Holy Spirit.

God has shown how much He loves us by forgiving sin when it is repented. In Isaiah 55:7, the Bible says, "Let the wicked forsake his way, and the unrighteous man his thoughts; and let him return to the Lord, and he will have compassion on him; and to our God, for he will abundantly pardon."

Put away competing and walking in selfishness in your marriage relationship. It is time to love and respect each other with the kind of love and respect that comes from God. It is time to pull each other up and not down.

Reflection

1. Read 1 Corinthians 13.

    Do a self-examination of your strengths and weaknesses according to 1 Corinthians13.

_____

_____

_____

_____

Pray that God will help you in the areas that you are weak in.

2. How can you love God's way?

_____

_____

_____

_____

_____

_____

_____

_____

3. How should a man love his wife?

_____

_____

_____

_____

_____

_____

_____

_____

4. How can you put the above into practice?_____

5. Have you surrendered your thoughts, feelings, emotions, and ideas about love to the Lord?

_____Yes _____No

6. What can you point to as evidence of the above?

_____

_____

_____

_____

_____

_____

CHAPTER 13

Unity and Harmony in the Home

One of the biggest problems in the home is the misuse of words. There is power in words. Words can have lasting effects. Name-calling and putting your spouse down is dangerous. For every idle word that we speak in our lifetime, we must give an account of it. Matthews 12:36–37 says, "But I say unto you, that every idle word that men shall speak, they shall give account thereof in the day of judgment. For by thy words thou shalt be justified, and by thy words thou shalt be condemned." The word "idle" means useless, wasteful, or barren. This means when we speak an idle word, we are speaking unfruitful, unspiritual, and unproductive words. It means that for every profane, obscene word or criticism that is spoken to your spouse, or anyone else, for that matter, you will give an account for it. Our words are very important because they are powerful. Proverbs 18:21 tells us, "Death and life are in the power of the tongue: and they that love it shall eat the fruit thereof." Your words have an impact whether you realize it or not. It is time for you to stop sabotaging your own life, family, and home. For when you call your spouse or your children some degrading name or walk around your home and speak curses, you are speaking death to your life and giving demons permission to tear your home down and to tear you and your family's lives down.

I have witnessed children being abused by their mothers because their mothers are angry with the children's fathers. And so they proceed to say things like, "Boy, you are lazy and no good just like your daddy," or fathers say to their daughters, "You are going to be a lazy woman just like your mother." When they become just like you prophesied, remember it is the curse that you spoke into their lives. If you do this, you are in partnership with Satan. You are just a tool for Satan to use to do his dirty work, accomplishing his purpose.

But the psalmist prays in Psalm 19:14, "That the words that come out of his mouth, and the thoughts that are constantly being reconciled and remembered in his heart, be acceptable in God's sight." In order to control your tongue and ultimately your words, you need strength from the Lord and you need Him to be your redeemer to deliver you from sin through your words. The psalmist calls out the titles of God reverently. And we have been made in His image and we should not call God's image degrading names. The psalmist says, "O Lord, my strength, and my redeemer." He calls on Jehovah the Lord, Jehovah his strength, and Jehovah his deliverer to help him watch his words. Because in order to control your tongue, or better your words, you need God as Lord of your life, you need strength from the Lord, and you need Him to be redeemer to deliver you from sin through your words. Ask God, "Let the words of my mouth, and the meditation of my heart, be acceptable in thy sight, O LORD, my strength, and my redeemer."

Ephesians 4:29 says, "Let no corrupt word proceed out of your mouth, but what is good or necessary for edification, that it may impart grace to the hearers." Think about the words you use on a day-to-day basis. What kind of attitude is being displayed when you speak to others? Are the words you use on a regular basis corrupt or unwholesome? What you should do is consider before you speak whether or not what you are about to say is going to give grace to those who hear.

Communication Is Vital to Harmony and Unity in Your Marriage

If a marriage is going to work, there must be communication. You can't live like a single person anymore because you are one with another person, and you must share your feelings and your thoughts.

Communication means coming together in honesty and openness. There are some guidelines for marital communication:

1. Find a quiet place to sit together.
2. Give each other your undivided attention.
3. If you feel angry, wait a while and just let the other one talk.
4. You should never use degrading language.
5. Pray together before a serious discussion.
6. Be careful about making blanket statements.
7. Never forsake saying "I am sorry," "Forgive me," or "I love you."

If a marriage is going to work, it must be according to God's design. God's design is one of partnership. You must remember that you are on the same team. Team members work together, not against each other.

In marriage God has given each party, the husband and the wife, a specific responsibility within their union. God did not create the struggles we see in marriage relationships today. He created unity in marriage and the family. It was not until the entrance of sin that unity was broken. When sin entered, there came a struggle. That is when they took on separate identities. In Genesis 3:20, the Bible says, "Now the man called his wife Eve; because she was the mother of all the living." Notice, she did not become "Eve" until after sin entered, because that original unity had been broken because of sin. Sin entered because they disobeyed God.

If we want unity in our families, we need to recognize three things.

1. We must agree to obey God's instructions.
2. We must agree to quit struggling with our God-assigned roles.
3. We must agree that sin is the blame, and Christ is the answer.

The husband is the head of the family, and the wife should not disrespect that. I have received and ministered to many women who say, "How can I respect a man who doesn't have a job, won't look for work, drink and takes drugs, persuades you to do drugs with him, beats you, and harasses the children all the time and hangs out with his friends all the time and is in and out of jail much of the time?" Well, I believe that it is obvious that this is not a man who is loving his wife as Christ loved the church. You have not been commanded to submit to the devil. A man that is a tool for the devil will not conform to the commands of God; thus, you do not have to submit to him. This man needs the space and time to seek pastoral counseling and then resume the duties of a husband once he understands what his responsibility is as a husband. The husband or head of household must learn how to subdue the earth, to have dominion over everything that moves on the earth. God instructed Adam to rule over the rest of creation. God delegated this authority to Adam in the beginning. He made Adam the head of household. After the fall Adam had to work. This means Adam had the responsibility to go out and hunt for food and chop down trees to make shelter for them to live. According to Gen 1:28–31, God blessed the man and woman with dominion over every living thing. The ruler of the universe saw it right to have men and women to serve as God's deputies over creation. God's goal for us men and women are to manifest God's righteous rule over all creation, and that mean we should start in our own families. Dominion doesn't mean men oppress women, nor women rebel against godly male leadership. Men and women are called to be disciples of Jesus Christ, and to disciple their children, so the earth can be filled with redeemed image bearers who wisely and justly manifest the Lord's sovereign holiness.

The Man of the house cannot hold up his role as delegated ruler of earth unless he is fixed on obeying God and depends on God's rule as king of all. If you want unity in the family, don't settle on staying in a rut. Seek God for directions and do what is best for you and your family in the eyes of God.

Unity can only be found when each spouse fulfills the role God has given him or her. In Genesis 2:20, the Bible says that there was no "helper similar to Adam until woman was fashioned." What does it mean to be a helper? It can be seen as the husband being the building, and the wife is the foundation to the building because she supports and encourages him. You don't tear down the building; you support and help the building to stand. You don't compete with the building; you do your job and let him do his. You don't hinder the building; you help the building. Because you are his helper, you are his friend. Jesus says in John 15:13, "Greater love has no one than this, that one lay down his life for his friends." A couple must also be friends as well as husband and wife. There must be agape love first of all, but there must also be Phileos love and eros love. The following are what a friend is not:

- A friend must not be in the relationship for self-gratification only.
- A friend is not in the relationship just for sex.
- A friend is not in the relationship to make a slave of the other.
- A friend is not in the relationship to dominate you, mistreat or abuse you.

The following are what a friend is:

- A friend is someone you can trust.
- A friend is someone you can laugh with, cry with, or rejoice with.
- A friend is someone that will be with you through all the trials and tribulations.

For unity in a marriage, a husband and wife should be friends as well as lovers, and a family united together in unconditional love also. And the only way to do this is to study the life of Christ Jesus and follow Him.

The family unity was broken because sin entered; it entered because Adam disobeyed God. Yet through Christ Jesus's redemptive work, we become "heirs together" of His grace. Christ has redeemed us, and if we want unity in our families, we must obey Christ Jesus.

Reflection

1. Study 1 Corinthians 7:3–5 and tell how you can keep unity in your marriage.

_____

_____

_____

_____

_____

_____

_____

_____

_____

2. First Corinthians 16:19 tells you that church was also held in the

_____

Thus, worship should start in the _____ of each family. You should be a member of a local church as well as practice worship in the family so that unity can prevail in the

_____.

3. Read Genesis 18:19 and discuss.

_____

_____

_____

_____

_____

_____

_____

_____

_____

_____

4. Second Timothy 1:5 tells us Timothy recalled the faith in and they were good models in the life of Timothy.

5. How can you keep eros, phileos, Storge, and agape love all alive and working together in your marriage.

CHAPTER 14

Cooperation Is the Key to Unity

The division that was taught by the slave owners during slavery was inhumane and evil. The division of people caused friction between groups of people according to how they were divided. Survival became more important than unity to the slaves. For instance, working in the master's house was more physically comfortable than working in the master's field. So those working in the master's house began to protect their positions by working against those in the fields. And as slavery technically ended, it left an aftermath of that same line of thought in the black race. For instance, the lighter-skinned blacks in some cases got better treatment and better chances in society, in such places as the school system and in the job market. Some of those who got a better chance took it at the expense of separating from the majority of blacks. All this brought on the bleak results of division. Division can be a learned behavior. Some learned behaviors spill over into the marriage relationship. Division is a difference of thought that causes dissension, disagreement, and disunion. While this is the rule for all races of people, it is the black man and black woman and their family that have been so cruelly divided during slavery. Thus, it would behoove the black man and black woman to look more closely at the order God instituted for the family to bring unity to the family.

Marriage and the family were founded by God. It is His divine creation, and it should not be tampered with. God knew just what order He wanted the family to live according to. And the order in which God designed the family to cohabit brings glory to Him. The very purpose of our lives is to bring glory to God. Thus, if we want unity in our families, our purpose must line up with God's purposes, and as it relates to God, that purpose must bring glory to God.

This should be of great interest to us, because when we really get into this, we make the happy discovery that we are to enjoy God and take delight in Him and in our relationship to Him.

In John 10:10b Jesus says, "I am come that they might have life, and that they might have it more abundantly." There is no way to have life abundantly unless you learn to come into the presence of God. In Psalm 16:11, David says, "Thou wilt show me the path of life: in thy presence is fullness of joy; at thy right hand there are pleasures for evermore." In Psalm 27:4b, the psalmist says, "That I may dwell in the house of the LORD all the days of my life, to behold the beauty of the LORD." In Psalm 73:25, Asaph cries out, "Whom have I in heaven but thee? And there is none upon earth that I desire beside thee." As it relates to the family, God wants unity! God wants you to enjoy Him! God wants you to delight in Him.

If you want unity in your family, there is a certain mode you must live in. You must:

1. Get into the presence of God!
2. Get into the permission of God!
3. Get into correct practice of the role God put you in!

- *In marriage, if you don't cooperate with God, you will never have unity.*
- *Unity will happen when we get into the presence of God.*

1. The best way to get into the presence of God is to humble yourself and submit to each other.
2. The best way to get into the presence of God is to pray together. A family that prays together, stays together. That is when you really surrender yourself to God together in prayer. When you pray together, you may hear what is on the other person's mind and come into agreement with that person, therefore promoting unity. Also, you will become closer to that person, because if the person is truly surrendered, you can begin to see the person's heart. When you begin to see into the person's heart, you will begin to empathize more with the person even when you are praying together. Communication can become clearer because of your new understanding of who the person really is. A family praying together is in the presence of God. What better presence can one get into?

- *In his presence, there is fullness of joy!*
- *In his presence, there is fellowship!*
- *In his presence, there is great blessing!*

The psalmist says in the Psalm 84, "How amiable are thy tabernacles, O Lord of Hosts! My soul longs, My soul longeth, yea, even fainteth for the courts of the LORD my heart and my flesh crieth out for the living God." And in verse 10, he says, "For a day in thy courts is better than a thousand."

When we begin to have tunnel vision for the Lord and not ourselves, the Holy Spirit will begin to:

- *Radiate in our actions!*
- *Radiate in our situations!*
- *Radiate in our speech!*
- *Radiate in our relationships!*

Woman/Wife

When we allow the Holy Spirit to conduct us, we begin to calm down and see things differently—that is, God's way. We become more cooperative, bringing unity into our marriages and our relationships in the family as a whole. Then, for example, if your husband asks you to make him that special meal, you won't immediately go off into some anger mode because you are in the presence of God, you have the mind of Christ, you understand what it is to be a Proverbs-31 woman, and you enjoy being an excellent wife because you are wise in the Lord. The Proverbs-31 woman is a blessed woman of God.

Man/Husband

If you want unity in the home, the home must be in order. This means that you must love your wife as Christ loves the church, which means you don't have to walk in a spirit of fear, because, according to 2 Timothy 1:7, "God has not given you a spirit of fear, but of power and of love and of a sound mind. Lean on Jesus to build you up in the Holy Spirit. He will anoint you and strengthen you with His redemptive love." You have to take care of your wife. This means that you must man up and get a job. You cannot hang out with your friends more than you hang out with your wife. If you cannot find a job, go back to school to get a higher education or a trade so that you can get a job or become an entrepreneur. But don't let the devil tell you that you cannot make it in life. Take your place in your marriage, in your family, and in society.

First Peter 3:7 instructs you to "live with your wives in an understanding way, as with a weaker vessel, since she is a woman; and grant her honor as a fellow heir of the grace of life, so that your *prayers* may not be hindered." This means that you should be harmonious, sympathetic, brotherly, kindhearted, and humble in spirit. It means that you should make sure that your wife is taken care of physically, emotionally, and spiritually.

Just like she should not always refuse to make you your special meal, by the same token, you should not always refuse to take her out to dinner. You should be happy to do so. And this doesn't mean going down to McDonald's either. If you can afford it, you need to take her to a nice restaurant with good service. Show her how much you appreciate her cooking that special meal for you. Don't let the trap that the devil has laid for you keep you from being the man and the head of the household.

Lonnie and Ma'kesha

Lonnie and Ma'kesha have been married for fifteen years, and out of that fifteen years, Lonnie has been in and out of prison most of the marriage, Ma'kesha has been the head of household for the duration of the marriage. Lonnie was institutionalized and didn't not know how to be helpful in this marriage. But together they decided to get Christian psychotherapy and pastoral counseling and as they completed counseling and seeking and surrendering God, their household began to work out according to the way God prescribed it to. Lonnie went back to school, graduated from college receiving a master's degree in business administration. He opened his own business and was very successful as an entrepreneur and real estate investor.

The prison system has a large number of black men locked up in prison for many different reasons. It is a continuation of slavery. It is learned dependency. And the one that has been locked up should not get out of prison and still act as if he or she is still in prison. Wake up. You are free! You are free to go to school and to get an education. You are free to form your own business. You are free to live a crime-free life. You are free to seek God! God can lead you in the right direction if you let Him.

- You are free to surrender all to God.
- You are free to love yourself, your wife, and family as God does.
- You are free to worship and fellowship with God.
- You are free to prosper

Marriage Reflects the Nature of God

The fact is that as men and women, we are equally important to God but we have different roles. You will have unity in your marriage if you know what your roles are and realize that your role is an important role. You will have unity in your marriage when you begin to "enter God's rest" in your specific roles by doing the following:

1. Being submissive.
2. Resting in the fact that your husband is your head just as Christ is his head.
3. Ceasing all rebellion.
4. Accepting the role God put you in.

You will have unity in your marriage if you are submissive to God and His will and submissive to your spouse.

In 1 Corinthians 7:3–4, the Bible instructs, "Let the husband render unto the wife due benevolence: and likewise also the wife unto the husband. The wife hath not power of her own body, but the husband: and likewise also the husband hath not power over his own body, but the wife." You must respond in a positive way. If you practice responding in a negative way, you will get a negative reaction, then you will get division in your relationship instead of unity.

Genesis 2:24 tells us, "Therefore a man leaves his father and mother and cleaves to his wife, and they become one flesh." This is not only a physical union; it is also speaking of a spiritual and emotional union of profound dimensions.

A husband and wife joined together in marriage are people that God has joined together. Jesus says in Matthew 19:6, "Consequently they are no longer two, but one flesh. What therefore God has joined together, let no man separate."

Sexual union with someone other than one's own wife or husband is a very seriously offensive kind of sin against one's own body. First

Corinthians 6:16 says, "Or do you not know that the one who joins himself to a harlot is one body with her? For he says, 'the two will become one flesh.'" If you have sexual relations outside your marital union, you have then become one with that person. You have violated the body of your spouse because 1 Corinthians 7:3–4 tells us husbands and wives no longer have exclusive rule over their own bodies because they share them with their spouses.

Marriage is a profound relationship created by God in order to picture the relationship between Christ and His church.

If a family enters submissiveness to God, prays together, correctly practices in the roles God has given each of them, enters God's presence, and enters God's rest in these, *unity will happen.*

Reflection

1. Read Mark 10:1–9. Name four basic guidelines for the marriage.

   a. _____

   _____

   b. _____

   _____

   c. _____

   _____

   d. _____

   _____

2. According to Mark 10:8, marriage is the only relationship that hold such high and vast closeness.

3. Marriage is the only relationship in which God views a husband and wife as _____.

    Husband and wife are unified as _____.

    The only way to have unity in a marriage is for each spouse to fulfill the role that God has _____.

4. What does Ephesians 5:25 say the husband's duty is to the wife?

    _____

    _____

    _____

5. What does Ephesians 5:22–24 say the wife's obligation to her husband is?

    _____

    _____

    _____

CHAPTER 15

Parenting for Unity in the Family

Ephesians 6:1–4 tells us, "Children, obey your parents in the Lord, for this is right. *Honor your father and mother,* (which is the first commandment with promise), *that it may be well with you, and that you may live long on the earth.* And, fathers, do not provoke your children to anger; but bring them up in the discipline and instruction of the Lord" (NAS).

One of the main reasons we don't see unity in the family is because some of the basic biblical principles and mandates that God has given us to live by have been neglected and sometimes downright ignored by families today. Basic biblical values that the family should live by have been destroyed by the adversary. In 2 Corinthians 2:11, Paul warns us not to be ignorant of the tricks of the devil.

Children are trying to identify with someone as they proceed to grow up. You should be the most impressive human role model in your child's life. If you allow the devil to influence your actions in the way you raise your child, you will be a total failure in the raising of your child.

You should be careful of what you say in front of your children. Cussing and fussing and using all kinds of profane and slang language in front of your children will spill over into their lives, and they will copy you and act the same way you do.

If you don't do anything but hang out with your friends or lay around the house all day and collect a welfare check, you can expect your child to do the same. And if all you do is play video games all day, It could possibly encourage your child to do the same thing. And if they grow up to live this way, it will be your fault and you will pay for it.

Keep unity in the family by practicing the following:

- practice avoiding the Devil's tricks.
- Practice raising your children according to the principles of the Word of God.
- teach your children to obey and respect you as their parent.

The worst thing to see is a child fussing back disrespectfully at their parents as if he was already grown. You must not allow your child to disrespect you in this way or any way. This is a trap of the devil. It is not cute. It is not cool. It is ignorant and degrading.

If we fall into his trap being willfully ignorant of him (the devil), he will find it very easy to take advantage of you with any one of his many deadly, destructive traps. One of his main goals is to destroy unity in the family. Your family, your home, is a field of attack for the devil, because if he can bring division into the household, he can begin to ruin the lives of your children. His goal is to try to keep generational curses prevailing in your family.

The devil is very real, and his goal is to kill you and your family. In Matthew 4:1–11, we find that Jesus and Satan had a face-to-face meeting. Jesus wasn't speaking to some nonexistent force. He was speaking directly to Satan. Satan has a personality: he can speak, he can act, he has emotions, and he has an intellect. And today, you will find him on some of the televisions shows, you will find him in some of the music, you will find him on the Internet. Just about anywhere you look, you will find him, because he is in competition with God for your life, for your children, and for your family. His intentions are to rob, steal, and kill you in the end.

It is most important that you begin to stand on the rock Jesus Christ and come under His authority, so that unity will take place in your home.

You should begin to speak the Word of God over your family.

1. I overcame by the blood of Christ and the word of my testimony! (Rev. 12:11)
2. The devil flees from me and my family because I resist him in Jesus's name! (James 4:7)
3. No weapon formed against me or my family shall prosper! (Isa. 54:17)
4. Great is the peace of my children for they are taught of the Lord. (Isa. 54:13)
5. You must begin to declare it and walk in it. Don't let Satan's goals come to pass in your home.

The world is dictating division in the family, and there is no blessing in it. All of a sudden they want to do things their way because the world has told them that their parents' ideas are too old fashioned. The peer pressure begins; and some parents begin letting the peer pressure cause them to change their God-given value system to Satan's value system and when this happens, in comes the family division. And there is no blessing in it.

While you are raising and teaching your children, it is not a good idea to allow them to sleepover at other people's homes, unless you know the people in that house very well. And if you do decide to allow your children to sleepover where you agree with the house rules and values of that family, the sleepover should be very well supervised. Proverbs 22:6 says, "Train up a child in the way he should go and even when he is old he will not depart from it." The Bible says in Joshua 24:15c, "But as for me and my house we will serve the Lord." You are stewards over your children and God expects you to be a good steward.

If children will obey their Christian parents, they will inherit generational blessings.

After Abraham obeyed God and after Isaac obeyed Abraham, God gave them a blessing; in Genesis 22:17–18, God tells Abraham, "Indeed I will greatly bless you, and I will greatly multiply your seed as the stars of the heavens, and as the sand which is on the seashore; your seed shall possess the gate of their enemies." Verse 18 says, "And in your seed all the nations of the earth shall be blessed, because you have obeyed my voice." Parents, remember, obedience brings blessings. You need to obey God, not the world! Not your children, nor your children's peers. The latest fad may not be what your children need to engage in. If you want to be blessed, you do as Abraham did: obey God. Parents must set good examples in the presence of their children. If they do, they will have a better chance for their children to be obedient. In Genesis 22:9–10, Abraham took his son Isaac up to the mountain as God instructed him as a sacrifice, trusting God to either provide another sacrifice or take his son as the sacrifice. He didn't question God; he obeyed God, and as a result, Isaac trusted and obeyed his father Abraham also. Abraham, being the head of household, a man of God, lived an upright life before God and his family. And the final result was a blessing. He trusted and obeyed the Lord, and as a result, the Lord provided a ram in the bush for Abraham.

As you live an upright life in the Lord, take care of your family, trust and obey God, you and your household will be blessed.

The instructions in Ephesians 6:1–4 is very simple.

- Obey your parents in the Lord. This means to hear your parents.

Obedience is a consequence of listening intently to the voice of God. For unity in the family, parents should make sure their household is run according to the principles of God and teach them to their children. How are children going to know this unless we teach them? A good prescription for unity in the family is for the head of household to lay down some dos and don'ts, some that we have already mentioned such as the following:Do bring the family together for a time of prayer, Bible study, and devotion.

- Do take the time to listen to your children's concerns too so that you can better address and advise them, and nurture and love them.
- Do communicate with your children.
- Don't just do all the dictating. Don't shut your child up all the time; listen to him or her.
- Don't provoke your child to anger.
- Don't call your child negative names.

Proverbs 18:21 says, "Death and life are in the power of the tongue, and they that love it will eat the fruit thereof." Speak blessings into your child's life. Speak words of encouragement; and God will bless you, your child, and your entire family. When you speak blessings to your child, you will be planting seeds of unity in your family and to the generations to come because your child will most likely speak blessings to his or her family also. Build generational blessings and not generational curses.

Reflection

Read Psalm 78:1–8.

According to Psalm 78, each generation seems to get worse and worse. What advice does the psalmist give you to help you in this generation?

_____

_____

_____

_____

_____

Read Psalm 139:13–16.

According to the scriptures, how well does God know our children?

_____

_____

_____

_____

_____

God has never made children to be mistakes: how does verse 14 say that he has made each child?

_____

_____

_____

_____

_____

_____ Read Matthew 22:37–38 and commit it to memory.

Obedience and a Full Love Barrel Is a Must

It is time for men and women to concentrate on rescuing their family. There is only one way to rescue your family from the destruction that has been planned for it, and that is by following the instructions of God. You have been misguided in family matters by the society in which you have found yourselves. Everyone is going to give an account to God for disobeying God. America will give an account for destroying black families in general. But you will give an account for destroying your family personally. It is time for you to take responsibility for your own actions. Dwelling on the blame game will not bring deliverance to you and your family. Understanding how you got to where you are is one thing, but doing something about it is another thing. You must take personal responsibility for your own actions *now*!

Achan's Disobedience Brings Destruction (Josh. 7:1–26)

Many black families have been able to stand and excel throughout the storm of oppression that has been placed on them by society. But for all intents and purposes, those families that are still breaking down and decaying from the demonic forces of this world need to know how to get off that path of destruction. Don't look for anyone else to rescue you and your family. You are the appointed one to do that under the instructions of God. If the head of the house is out of order, the entire household is going to be affected. And by the same token, if even one household in the black community is out of order, the entire black community is affected.

In verse 24, we find that Achan got his whole family killed because of his disobedience, his greed, and, overall, his sin. What happened to Achan's family is still very relevant in families today. That is why the entire black community need to be in prayer, need to witness, need to mentor and evangelize, equip and empower as many as possible. Jesus is the answer. Second Corinthians 5:17 tells us, "Therefore if any man be in Christ, he is a new creature: old things are passed away; behold, all things are become new."

In the KJV Bible, the word "household" can be found sixty-one times. The word "household" is an important word because it covers everyone living in a particular house. It is not limited to the nuclear family. It covers multigenerational families, single-parent families, as well as two-parent families. What the Bible teaches about "households" is relevant to and for everyone. Achan is an example of how you can bring destruction to your entire household. It clearly teaches that if you neglect your spiritual responsibility, you will bring chaos into your household. Achan was in deep sin, and his sin centers around "the accursed things." Joshua 7:1 states, "But the children of Israel committed a trespass regarding the accursed things, for Achan took of the accursed things; so the anger of the LORD burned against the children of Israel."

When you make a conscious decision to disobey God and do what pleases you, you open the door to your own destruction. Joshua told his army about the expected victory at Jericho, and he gave them orders and instruction on what to do and what to expect. In Joshua 6:17–19, he instructed them, "And the city shall be accursed, even it, and all that are therein, to the LORD: only Rahab the harlot shall live, she and all that are with her in the house, because she hid the messengers that we sent. And ye, in any wise keep yourselves from the accursed thing, lest ye make yourselves accursed, when ye take of the accursed thing, and make the camp of Israel a curse, and trouble it. But all the silver, and gold, and vessels of brass and iron, are consecrated unto the LORD: they shall come into the treasury of the LORD." Some things belong to God. The head of household should never keep that which belongs to God, for when he does, he brings a curse on his household. As Malachi 3:8 tells you, you are robbing God when you don't tithe. The first 10 percent does not belong to you; and you have been instructed, just as Achan was instructed, to not take what belonged in God's treasury. Achan wasn't willing to give God what belong to Him. Men should always say and do as Joshua said, "As for me and my house, we will serve the Lord (Josh. 24:15c)." A self-serving man will not be concerned with his household, only with himself. Anyone who is self-serving will not be concerned with praying and obeying God. Women living in a household with a self-serving husband can only survive if they are submitted to God and if they are prayer warriors. As they pray and intercede, their husbands can become submitted to God through their influence. If intercessory prayer is constant in the home of a self-serving man, it can and will save the home from destruction.

Another reason destruction came up on Achan's household is because he was not only self-serving; he sinned and tried to hide his sin. Joshua 7:21 tells us, "When I saw among the spoils a beautiful Babylonian garment, two hundred shekels of silver, and a wedge of gold weighing fifty shekels, I coveted them and took them. And there they are, hidden in the earth in the midst of my tent, with the silver under it." The problem with Achan is that he was trying to hide his sin from God. How foolish can you get? You cannot hide sin from God. The best thing to do is to admit it and repent of it before it is too late.

Repentance is necessary. God already knows. Disobedience brings a curse on you and your household. Numbers 32:23c says, "Be sure your sin will find you out."

It is time to remember that God is the one who brought you out of slavery and God is the only one who can keep you out of spiritual slavery.

In Exodus 20:2, God graciously loved Israel and helped Israel leave Egypt, yet Israel responded with rebellion. They chose new gods, violating the most basic responsibility of their covenant relationship with God. In verse 3, God tells them, "Thou shalt have no other gods before me," yet as soon as they were freed, they turned on God. Black men and black women, instead of imitating white America, you should be imitating Jesus. You should be promoting the word of God in your community instead of promoting the sale of illegal drugs and idolizing automobiles, gold necklaces, and other jewelry, and competing in material things. You are free to worship God, not things, and when you realize this, you will walk in the blessings of God in great abundance in your household and in your community, for the Bible says in Matthew 6:33, "But seek ye first the kingdom of God, and His righteousness; and all these things shall be added unto you." This dog-eat-dog world would say to seek things first, but this is a lie and a trick from the devil, and when you imitate this, you are in for destruction.

Before There Can be Restoration, There Must Be Repentance

The Bible tells us in Hosea 14:2–4, "Take with you words, and turn to the LORD: say unto him, Take away all iniquity, and receive us graciously: so will we render the calves of our lips. Asshur shall not save us; we will not ride upon horses: neither will we say any more to the work of our hands, ye are our gods: for in thee the fatherless findeth mercy. I will heal their backsliding, I will love them freely: for mine anger is turned away from him." In order for God to forgive and restore your family, you must understand and admit that you have sinned, and when you ask for forgiveness and mean it in your heart, the Lord will forgive you. God wants unblemished words from our hearts that offer praises to Him.

God did not want Israel to depend on the nation Assyria or their own army's ability to save them. It was time for Israel to give up her love for man-made idols as her god. It was high time for her to understand and believe that because God had compassion for the orphan, He would have compassion for Israel. God will shower blessings on you when you repent.

Repentance always comes from the heart before it can come through the lips. In Matthew 12:34b, Jesus says, "For out of the abundance of the heart the mouth speaketh." In Hosea 14:1, God invites them to "return unto the LORD thy God; for thou hast fallen by thine iniquity." The price to be paid is confession of sins. When we turn from the world, we become strangers of the world. When we turn to God, we have ownership of a new life.

God has chosen the black man and black woman to teach the world about how God has strengthened them to come out of slavery and live in a world of discrimination, rejection, and continue to receive harsh treatment and still survive.

God told the prophet Hosea to marry and give his love to a prostitute. She continued to be unfaithful to him, yet each time she was unfaithful, God told Hosea to take her back and love her. This is symbolic of God giving His love to His people even if they are unfaithful to Him. Even when they disregard His love over and over again, He pursues them. God's love is a permanent love. You may ask, "Should I seek to marry an active prostitute?" No! I don't believe this is the point here. I believe that God is telling us that there is some risk involved in loving another person. Knowing love at its deepest level involves risk. You risk every time you give your love because you don't know how it will be returned to you. But if you never allowed yourself to love out of fear, you would never know what it was to love another person. I believe God is telling you that you will have to put up with something because no one can completely meet the needs of another human being. God is the only one perfect and the only one we can draw on to fill up our love barrels.

There is no perfect person. If you married a bad cook, or your spouse gained weight, or is not as attractive as he or she was when you married her/him, you must stay in the marriage and learn how to love an imperfect person because you are imperfect yourself. When you vowed before God to marry for better or for worse, this meant that you would not pack up and leave as soon as things stopped looking like you want them to. Marriage can only be redemptive when you learn to love an imperfect person.

Can You Receive Love?

Love is a two-way street. You have to allow yourself to be loved in order for love to take place. You will never be a recipient of love if you reject all the love that is sent to you. You must know that you are worth love from another person. If you feel so unlovable, it means that you think that love has a price tag on it and you cannot measure up to the price tag. Some people feel so inadequate they believe they have to pay for love. True love cannot be bought. If you will not allow God to penetrate you with his love, you will not be able to receive nor give love to anyone. Some people have gone so long without love they have become immune to love.

A Redemptive Relationship Requires a Full Love Barrel

The only completely full love barrel is God. You can draw off God's love to fill your love barrels, and in doing this, you can give love to those in your circle. As Hemfelt, Minirth, and Meier state, "Our love is flawed; His is perfect. Ours has limits: His does not. Ours depends upon the response we receive; He acts in our best interests whether we requite His love or not. We cannot make each other happy; He can. He is the Ultimate source of nurturing" (Hemfelt, Minirth, and Meier 1989). People who are suffering from hurt, abuse, and oppression can find restoration by drawing off the limitless supply of love from God.

Prayer Father God, in the name of Jesus Christ, I am sorry for my sins and I come before You confessing my sins of omission and commission, and also the sins of (name them here)

I surrender my life completely to You. And I ask You to be my savior. Please rest, rule, and abide in me as I abide in You and Your words abide in me. Help me each day to follow Your directions. Help me to decrease as You increase in me. I open myself to You and ask You to pour Your undying love into me that I may be able to pour it out to all in my household as well as all those I come in contact with. Please restore me and my household. Amen.

Reflection

1. Read Hosea 14:2 and discuss how repentance comes.

_____

_____

_____

_____

_____

_____

2. Read Hosea 14:4 and discuss.

_____

_____

_____

_____

_____

_____

3. Read Joshua 7:24–26 and discuss the consequence that Achan brought on his whole family.

_____

_____

_____

_____

_____

_____

4. What could you do to alleviate deadly consequences in your family?

_____

_____

_____

_____

_____

_____

5. Read and meditate on the Psalm 51, 1 Peter 4:17, 1 Corinthians 11:28, Matthew 7:1–5, Psalms 139:23, 1 John 1:9, John 8:28– 32, and James 5:16.

6. You can always draw from God if you totally depend on Him to fill up your love barrel. You cannot love and trust anyone until you first love and trust God. It is God that will help you to have healthy relationships with others. Share the love you receive from your relationship with Jesus and with others to bring about redemptive relationships.

7. Read Philippians 2:13 and discuss.

_____

_____

_____

_____

_____

_____

CHAPTER 17

What the Bible Says about Courtship

The only way to know what and how God thinks about the subject of courtship is by reading what he says about it in the Bible. The Song of Solomon will reveal to you that love, romance, sex, and passion are fine in a relationship based on commitment, integrity, and honesty, if it is involved in holy matrimony.

Love and romance, sex and passion are not meant to be lasting when it is entailed in a relationship that is out of order with God. Sex is out of order in a relationship when it is done in fornication, and there is no blessing on it. Yet a vast number of black men and black women live together in sin. They call it shacking up. Some may say, "So what! Everybody is doing it." My response to you is, two wrongs don't make a right. You don't just jump off into a firepit just because everybody else is doing it. That would be foolish to say the least. I have spent years interviewing men and women who found themselves shacking up, and some of the reasons they say they shack up are as follows:

- I don't want my welfare check cut off or monitored more closely.
- I don't want to go through the time, expense, or effort to get a divorce if the relationship doesn't work out.

- I'm already married to someone else and don't want to go through the court procedure because of child support issues.

These are a few of the excuses that have been given to me as to why some don't want or can't get married to the partner they are with. But if you want a blessed relationship, you must do it right. You must trust God and do it the way God wants you to do it. You do not have to live together. Why would you want to live in sin? How are you going to repent if you are living in it continuously? Don't allow the devil to trick you and rob you of the blessing that God has for you. If you base your relationship on the way God sees a relationship, blessings will flow in your relationship.

During the courtship process, you should decide whether or not this is a person that you can or cannot marry. If it is not, you should cut off the courtship immediately; otherwise, why are you courting the person?

Does He/She Stink or Smell Pleasant?

The Bible says in Song of Solomon 1:1–3, "Let him kiss me with the kisses of his mouth for your love is better than wine. Because of the fragrance of your good ointments, your name is ointment poured forth; therefore, the virgins love you." The kissing is indicative of reconciliation and restoration to favor, as in the case of Esau kissing Jacob in Genesis 33:4 and the father of the prodigal son kissing his returning son in Luke 15:20, and will be when the Jewish remnant and the Gentiles "kiss the Son" in kingdom blessing (Ps. 2:12) (Unger 2002).

The Shulamite gave high regard to Solomon, and she wanted to kiss him, not because she was seeking some sexual arousal or physical/mental gratification, but because she believed his name was so respectful and of such high integrity. She was aware of the sweet aroma of the Lord on Solomon.

What kind of aroma do you present within the courtship process? Do you stink with bad language, manipulation, possessiveness, immoral behavior, jealousy, argumentative, etc.; or do you present a sweet aroma that could only come from the Lord? That is, the sweetness of selflessness, helpfulness, moral conduct, integrity, respect, etc.

Walking with Satan and the world in your life will give off a stinking aroma because the aroma of the world is an aroma produced by Satan. It can be detected in a person's words and deeds. There will be no integrity in the person; however, you should allow the Holy Spirit to guide you in your decision. Pray for the gift of discernment, because Satan is a liar and a grand counterfeiter.

What Is a Person of Integrity?

- A person of integrity will be a person that will have steadfast adherence to a strict moral or ethical code.
- A person of integrity walks in completeness, unified in the Lord.
- A person of integrity's words and deeds will not be different; they will match up; he/she will not be a hypocrite.
- A person of integrity will not be phony, dishonest, and double-minded.

- A person of integrity will be single-minded, because his/her thoughts are Godward, striving to have the mind of Christ.

- "Integrity is not what we do so much as who we are. Our system of values is so much a part of us we cannot separate it from ourselves. It becomes the navigating system that guides us" (Maxwell 1993).

Moreover, true and lasting integrity comes from allowing the Holy Spirit to lead, guide, and direct you in everything you do or say, because there is no good thing in the flesh. It is only when we have surrendered our lives wholly to the Lord Jesus that we can be whole and single-minded.

In Solomon's day, you had to bathe yourself in perfume to take away the stink of the day. Today, you must bathe yourself in the perfume of Jesus Christ, which is the only way to have a sweet aroma that will get the attention of those who are seeking to be in a relationship with a person who is walking in the righteousness of Jesus Christ.

The Shulamite woman was saying to Solomon that he has a sweet aroma, he got her attention. She had checked around about him (she asks the maidens about him) and he had a respected name that was like a sweet perfume. She was certain she would appreciate and like his courtship.

Proverbs 22:1 tells us, "A good name is rather to be chosen than great riches, and loving favour rather than silver and gold."

It is beneficial for the black man and the black woman to hold to a strict moral and ethical code that will produce blessings in their lives and those of their children and their children's children. The Bible is your guide. Do not pick and choose which morals and ethics you want to follow as they have been taught to you by Western society. You are free to be steadfast, immovable, and abounding in the Lord, who will teach you and point you to integrity.

Black Women

Just as the Shulamite woman knew of Solomon as a man of integrity, you should allow the Lord to show you the man of integrity for your life partner. The man of integrity may not be the man with what you may call "good hair or lighter skin." Come out of slavery. You are still in slavery when you believe what the white society has taught you about skin color and hair. This is one of the ways to end up with the wrong marriage partner. He may be the very one that will abuse you and not provide for you and your children. No matter how pretty you may think those children may be, they need food to eat and a roof over their heads, and a father that will work and love them and not just his "pretty self."

If you want someone that will last, someone that you will be happy with for the rest of your life, someone to give your children love, respect, and care for them, start dating a person of integrity, then marry a person of integrity. Proverbs 20:6 instructs us, "Many a man claims to have unfailing love, but a faithful man who can find?"

A faithful man is a man of integrity. The courtship process is very important. If you court long enough, you are bound to find out something about the man you are courting. So it behooves you to wait long enough before you marry him. I don't believe you will ever find a person who will say, "I am so glad I married this man who physically, mentally, emotionally, and verbally abuses me" or "I love the way this man puts me down and gets angry at me at the drop of a hat." Proverbs 20:6 is telling you that you can have the most eloquent, cool, calm, and collected-acting person that will sweep you off your feet, yet abuse you worst than you could ever imagine behind closed doors. A really smooth sweet talker always says those things that just about make you faint, but it should not be words that draw you close to this person; it should be actions that draw you close to him. Let's get real and understand that to find that faithful person is difficult, yet it is not impossible. The Bible tells us in Matthew 19:26b, "But with God all things are possible," and in Genesis 18:14a, "Is anything too difficult for the Lord?" This is why you should never attempt to do dating and courtship or marriage on your own, but with God only.

When you attempt to do it on your own, Satan will get in and blind you for sure, and you could ruin not only your own life but your children's and your children's children lives. Don't you think this is too high of a price to pay, just because you did what your flesh wanted you to do?

In Song of Solomon 1:5–7, the Shulamite woman says, "I am black, but comely, O ye daughters of Jerusalem, as the tents of Kedar, as the curtains of Solomon. Look not upon me, because I am black, because the sun hath looked upon me: my mother's children were angry with me; they made me the keeper of the vineyards; but mine own vineyard have I not kept. Tell me, O thou whom my soul loveth, where thou feedest, where thou makest thy flock to rest at noon: for why should I be as one that turneth aside by the flocks of thy companions?" She is saying that although she has not been able to take care herself for taking care of the fields, she is still black and beautiful, and she is not ashamed of who she is. She knows she is "fearfully and wonderfully made" (Ps. 139:14b).

The Uniqueness of the Black Women

You should recognize that the black woman is "fearfully and wonderfully made," a rarity among women. Who could have endured the brutal treatment that she has? During slavery, she had to endure carrying children in her womb that were forcefully put there through rape, yet she bore the children of rape and loved them anyway. She continued living and working and serving and watching her daughters go through the same treatment. She continued, even though she had no husband to protect her or provide for her because her husband had been taken from her through death or by the slave trade, sold to a place of no return. She learned to be tough. And even in modern-day slavery, she has had to learn to be tough because her husband may be in jail or prison or a runaway man who ran because of unemployment or learned behavior that is not so easily unlearned. But if it had not been for the Lord on her side, where would she be? Proverbs 31:30 tells us, "Favour is deceitful, and beauty is vain: but a woman that feareth the LORD, she shall be praised." It is a shame to belittle her and compare her to what the media calls a woman.

In Song of Solomon 1:9 the Bible says, "I have compared thee, O my love, to a company of horses in Pharaoh's Chariots." Solomon is not calling her a horse. He is saying that the pharaoh's horse would be the one symbol of power when the pharaoh was out. The pharaoh would have pride in it. It would be the sleekest, the fastest, the best-looking horse anywhere in that part of the world. He is saying he is proud of her just as she is. She also states that her blackness is beautiful in Song of Solomon 1:5, "I am black, but comely, O ye daughters of Jerusalem, as the tents of kedar, as the curtains of Solomon."

Song of Solomon 2:4 says, "He brought me to the banqueting house, and his banner over me was love." This is saying that instead of going on a walk on the beach, he brings her home to meet everyone in the house so that everyone can see who this person is, especially those that don't have rose-colored glasses on. It is a time when everyone should see who this important person in your life is. In Solomon's time, when a king would go out to battle, he would put a flag out with his colors or a name on it so that his soldiers would know where their leader was. This woman should be saying that she knows that she belongs to him because of their love for each other in all that she does and says while she is with everyone in the house. It should be seen when they come into the room just by what he does for her and how she reacts with everyone in the house. He accepts her as one of his family, and she accepts him with his family.

Song of Solomon 2:7 tells us, "I charge you, O ye daughters of Jerusalem, by the roes, and by the hinds of the field, that ye stir not up, nor awake my love, till he pleases." Do not defile the purity of your wife to be. Leave her a virgin. Solomon is saying not to push the woman you love into sex before marriage. He is saying *wait*. He is stepping up to the plate and saying, "No, not right now. This will have to wait until we are married." He doesn't let her push him into it either. He is saying he understands how she feels, but as a leader, he must lead her right. This indicates that Solomon is a man of integrity!

Traditionally, most of the time, it is the women that say no. However, we are living in times when many women are willing to say yes. But you must be men of integrity because you are the leaders.

Song of Solomon 2:11–14 tells us, "For, lo, the winter is past, the rain is over and gone; The flowers appear on the earth; the time of the singing of birds is come, and the voice of the turtle is heard in our land; The fig tree putteth forth her green figs, and the vines with the tender grape give a good smell. Arise, my love, my fair one, and come away. O my dove, that art in the clefts of the rock, in the secret places of the stairs, let me see thy countenance, let me hear thy voice; for sweet is thy voice, and thy countenance is comely."

This is saying that during courtship, you need to talk about the good and bad. This means that you will talk about those subjects that are difficult as well as the nice and easy subjects. The reason is that you need to find out how you communicate when a difficult subject is talked about or whether or not you can communicate at all.

Communication and money are two of the top reasons for divorce in the United States. Why go further than the courtship if you cannot communicate within the courtship relationship? That is a big *stop sign*.

Song of Solomon 2:15 tells us, "Take us the foxes, the little foxes, that spoil vines: for our vines have tender grapes." This tells you that you should take the relationship seriously and make sure that sin does not destroy your relationship. This woman knew about something that could destroy a vineyard. What is being said here is that you should be careful to not allow anything to wreck this relationship.

Proverbs 28:13 tells you, "He that covereth his sins shall not prosper: but whoso confesseth and forsaketh them shall have mercy."

There is no point in keeping things from your fiancée. The courtship period is the time to be honest. There is no better time to be honest other than the period of courtship. It is best for you to be honest with yourself, your fiancée, and, most of all, with God.

Reflection

Does the person you are dating have integrity? If so, can you identify it?

_____

_____

_____

_____

_____

Write out Proverbs 20:6 and memorize it.

_____

_____

_____

_____

Read Proverbs 31:30 and write what it means to you and tell how it can benefit you.

_____

_____

_____

_____

What does Proverbs 22:1 tell you to look for during courtship?

_____

_____

_____

_____

_____

According to Proverbs 24:26, you should be looking for an answer.

CHAPTER 18

All Promiscuity Must End

Hebrews 13:4 says, "Marriage is honourable in all, and the bed undefiled: but whoremongers and adulterers God will judge. However, everyone has some kind of past and all God ask for is repentance. Let your past go and move on and upward. We serve a forgiving God. 1 John 1:9 tells us, "if we confess our sins, he is faithful and just to forgive us our sins, and to cleanse us from all unrighteousness." This means, God love us so much that all we have to do is bring it to him and leave it there."

Living a life of promiscuity can mean physical death or broken fellowship with God. The consequences are tremendous. Sexually transmitted diseases of all types are harmful; however, AIDS is claiming more black lives than any other group.

God has given us the perfect plan for sex, and that plan includes one man and one woman within the marriage relationship. Millions of dollars will be spent this year on sex education, which, by the way, has the wrong answer that is called safe sex. This is a lie from the enemy. The only safe sex is the sex prescribed in God's plan. God's prescription for safe sex is abstinence until marriage. First Peter 2:11

tells us, "Dearly beloved, I beseech you as strangers and pilgrims, abstain from fleshy lusts, which war against the soul." God tells us that safe sex wars against your soul. Worldly safe sex fights against you, not with you.

Promiscuity means sleeping around with whomever you want. In 1 Corinthians 6:15–18, Paul tells Christians, "Know ye not that your bodies are the members of Christ? Shall I then take the members of Christ, and make them the members of a harlot? God forbid. What?

Know ye not that he which is joined to a harlot is one body? For two, saith he, shall be one flesh. But he that is joined unto the Lord is one spirit. Flee fornication. Every sin that a man doeth is without the body; but he that committeth fornication sinneth against his own body." God is telling you to run quickly from sexual immorality. Whomever you have sex with, you become one with that person, which means you are having sex with every sexual partner that the person has had sex with.

Verse 19 says, "What? know ye not that your body is the temple of the Holy Spirit which is in you, which ye have of God, and ye are not your own?"

Immorality and untamed lust are condemned by God because they are evil and bring destruction into the lives of all those involved. Samson is a prime example of how promiscuity can destroy your life. Yes, we see lives being destroyed each day with sexually transmitted deceases, marriages being destroyed, yet this is not a surprise. God has left us the reminder in His Holy Scriptures. Samson became a womanizer and lived a promiscuous life.

Samson was infatuated and in lust with the woman of Timnah. Samson was filled with lust for the prostitute in Gaza. Samson fell in love with Delilah.

Playing with the fire of promiscuity deceived him into giving his heart to the lethal weapon, Delilah, the one who would do anything for money. Samson became putty in the hands of this lethal weapon, who was a devil out to kill him in the beginning. But Samson was blinded by sin. Sin is known to blind those who play around with it. Many were born to be prophets, teachers, pastors, evangelists, apostles, and men of God, leading your families into the house of God to bring glory to God; yet you have gone from pleasing God to pleasing Satan. The Philistines knew that Samson liked to dance, so they got Delilah, who loved to dance too. The devil is watching your every move, your every word and action. He is studying you so that he can move in and hit right on target. If you allow immorality to enter or dominate your eye gate or ear gate, it can blind you and lead you in the wrong direction. Satan was targeting Samson for spiritual blindness first. After he accomplished spiritual blindness, he then moved in for physical blindness. Lustful eyes only see the pleasure of the night, not the transmitted disease that will cause you to live a physically, emotionally, and spiritually painful life and then die a painful death.

Delilah is the promiscuous woman that will do anything for some money. She will become sexually involved with your friends, relatives, or whoever will supply her gold-digging desires. *Stay away from her.* Nobody can supply your need and give you a peace as the Lord can. After Delilah stabbed Samson in the back (metaphorically speaking), his strength left him and the saddest thing happen to him, and that is, the Lord left him. In Judges 16:20c, the Bible says, "And he wist not that the LORD was departed from him." This is the conclusion that the devil has for you. Promiscuity is a lethal weapon, the lethal weapon of being separated from God. It is the lethal weapon of HIV and AIDS and other sexually transmitted disease that will make you live like a leper.

Once you have repented and given your life to Christ, you have been cleansed by the blood of Christ Jesus. Then you can take the commandment to honor God with your body and convert it into the reality of how you live your life.

Practical Things to Do to Evade Promiscuity

1. Protect your mind. Put a guard over your eye gate and your ear gate because they are roadways to the mind. Second Peter 2:14 tells us, "Having eyes full of adultery, and that cannot cease from sin; beguiling unstable souls; a heart they have exercised with covetous practices; cursed children." Protect your children by repenting of all sinful lifestyles.
2. Don't accommodate sin.
3. Don't date anyone who will pressure you into a sexual encounter: "But put ye on the Lord Jesus Christ, and make no provision for the flesh, to fulfill the lusts thereof" (Rom. 13:14).
4. You should learn to recognize and flee from any situation that would lead you into temptation.

5. You must commit yourself to live a holy life. First Peter 1:15–16 says, "But as he which hath called you is holy, so be ye holy in all manner of conversation; Because it is written, Be ye holy; for I am holy" (KJV).

6. Commit yourself to daily Bible reading, meditation, and prayer.

7. Remove all ungodly, sexually immoral, and sexually explicit materials from your midst.

8. Enlist accountability partners, people that you promise to confess sexually immoral sins to. These should be people that you give authority to question you about your sexual purity at any time.

9. Seek to serve God and become a witness for God.

10. Pray that God send you your life mate.

Reflection

1. Read Romans 13:13–14 and discuss what it means to behave properly.

---

2. Read Galatians 5:16–18.How should you walk and why?

_____

_____

_____

_____

_____

_____

_____

_____

3. Read Galatians 5:19–26 and examine yourself as to your flesh and as to your fruit.

_____

_____

_____

_____

_____

_____

_____

_____

4. Read Genesis 1:27–28 and 2:24–25 and explain what it means to you.

_____

_____

_____

_____

_____

_____

_____

_____

_____

5. Read Proverbs 5:15–20 and state how sexual love is to be enjoyed.

_____

_____

_____

_____

_____

_____

_____

_____

6. Read 1 Corinthians 7:3–5 and state what responsibility the husband and wife have in sexual love.

_____

_____

_____

_____

_____

_____

CHAPTER 19

You Must Endure

Child of God, God does not want you to lose hope. He wants you to run this race like you are a winner. And you can only be a winner if you are in Christ. You cannot run the race alone. A redemptive marital relationship is only possible through Christ Jesus. In Philippians 4:13, Paul tells us, "I can do all things through Christ who strengthens me." This is the only way to endure the trials and tribulations that we will encounter. When Jesus said in the gospel of John 14:30 that the ruler of this world was coming, he did not mean that Satan was coming for the first time, because Satan was not appearing for the first time. All through Jesus's ministry here on earth, the devil came and tried to tempt and oppose Him bitterly and consistently through various ways. And the same will continue to happen to us too. But you too must endure to the end.

In 2 Timothy 2:3–5, the Bible says, "You therefore must endure hardship as a good soldier of Jesus Christ. No one engaged in warfare entangles himself with the affairs of this life, that he may please him who enlisted him as a soldier. And also if anyone competes in athletics, he is not crowned unless he competes according to the rules" (NKJV).

You must understand that the Christian life is the best privilege one can have; at the same time, you must also understand that the Christian life is warfare, not a picnic. There are battles to be fought, enemies to be conquered, and victories to be won. And yes, there are wonderful feasts to be enjoyed all along the way; but fighting, not feasting, should be your special business. Fighting in the spirit is your duty. Second Corinthians 10:4 tells us, "The weapons of our warfare are not carnal, but are mighty through God to the pulling down of strongholds." This simply means that human methods will not help. We cannot defeat the devil arguing, having the last word, fistfighting, or using guns and knives. The weapons of the word of God will defeat the devil. A soldier must continue to fight, even when the odds look like they are against him/her.

Just as Paul charges Timothy to endure to the end, God has charged every Christian to endure to the end also. Black men and black women, God wants you to be a winner, just as Paul wanted Timothy to be a winner. He wants you to persevere. But in order to be a winner, you must be consistent.

- Be consistent in how you think!
- Be consistent in how you talk!
- Be consistent in your faithful walk with the Lord.

You cannot win the fight for your family if you don't endure. If one minute you want to be a husband and father, wife and mother and the next minute you are ready to throw in the towel, will not seek counseling, will not talk to the pastor, and will not even talk to God, you are then a loser of the worst kind. *No! No! No! You must endure to the end.* You must set plans according to God's will for your life and have faith in God to carry them out through you. If you are consistent and obedient and if you will endure to the end, *you can make it.*

How Do You Endure to the End?

- When God says change, you change!
- When God says seek wise counsel, you seek wise counsel! Proverbs 24:6 says, "For by wise counsel thou shalt make thy war; and in multitude of counsellors there is safety."
- When God says go, you go.

No matter how impossible things may look, obey God! Fight the good fight of faith, and God will bring you through.

When we look up "fight" in the Greek, we find that "fight" means to literally consume, to overcome. And you are an overcomer in Jesus Christ.

There will be ups and downs. Joshua went through ups and downs, but he never gave up. He endured, and the result was ultimately victory.

Joshua

- Victory at Jericho (up) (chap. 6)
- Defeat at Ai (down) (chap. 7)
- Victory at Ai (up) (chap. 8)
- Failure with the Gibeonites (down) (chap. 9)
- Victory over the Amorites (up) (chap. 10)
- Victory over the no. Canaans (up) (chap. 11)
- Victory over all the kings (up) (chap. 12)

Never, never give up! Fight the good fight of faith, knowing that God is able to deliver. Obey God. Do your part and God will do His part.

There are four things you need to know if you want to fight the good fight.

1. Know your enemy.
2. Know how to fight him.
3. Know the conditions to succeed in your warfare.
4. Who and what is it that you are to fight?

Your husband/wife/family is not your enemy!

1. It is the devil. Ephesians 6:11–12 tells us, "Put on the full armor of God, that you may be able to stand firm against the schemes of the devil. For our struggle is not against flesh and blood, but against the world forces of this darkness, against the spiritual forces of wickedness in the heavenly places" (NAS). What I want you to understand about this is that the devil wants to hold you bound in his jail, as his prisoner under his legal authority. The legal authority the devil has over someone that enables him to hold him/her bound is called a principality—a powerful ruler or the rule of someone in authority. The word may refer to human rulers (Tit. 3:1, KJV; demonic spirits [Rom. 8:38, Eph. 6:12, Col. 2:15]; angels and demons in general [Eph. 1:21, Col. 2:10]). The territory or jurisdiction of a prince is the country that gives title to a prince. The devil is the prince of the air (Eph. 2:2). The word "title" means ownership, claim, right. It comprises all the

elements constituting legal ownership that are a legally just cause of exclusive possession. When the devil develops a principality in our minds or our bodies, he produces what is called a stronghold.

Because of strongholds, the black man and the black woman and their relationship is suffering in hurt and pain. And it is being perpetuated when children are left to grow up in broken or loveless homes. When this brokenness and boundedness is perpetuated in the home, children grow up as cast-offs, rejects. Some are no longer seen as viable members of society. This stronghold will produce adults that have no direction in their lives, wandering about aimlessly, confused and perplexed. They are being incarcerated mentally, physically, and spiritually in the most cruel and ultimately eternal prison. Satan has sentenced them with a life sentence of emotional emasculation, depression, anxiety, low or no self-esteem, and fear. Many are living on a spiritual death row because of the addiction to deadly narcotics, alcohol, promiscuity, uninhibited sexual activity, all to numb the pain they feel from the devil's stronghold. Many are being held captive to physical pain and discomfort from disease. They are being held in these seemingly inescapable prison bars, spiritually lost, wandering about through life hopelessly, just waiting to die. What they have experienced to be life is something they hope will be over soon. What they don't understand is that Jesus has already paid the price for their freedom. All they have to do is come. There is an answer that will produce life.

Repent and be baptized in the name of Jesus and be filled with the Holy Ghost, because true deliverance can only be found by fixing your eyes on the face of God and asking Him to intercede for you.

Be clearly informed that alcohol, depression, narcotics, and illicit sexual activity are only the manifestations of the true bondage, which is the bondage of the mind. The Bible tells us in Proverbs 23:7a, "For as a man thinketh in his heart, so is he." The devil knows that the way a person thinks is how a person will act. The drug-addicted, the sex-addicted, the alcohol–addicted person thinks he or she needs it in order to make it through, when actually these are just demonic suggestions and insistence from the devil through his or her mind. It is bondage of the mind, all manufactured by the devil.

The Bible tells us in Romans 12:2, "And be not conformed to this world: but be ye transformed by the renewing of your mind, that ye may prove what is that good, and acceptable, and perfect will of God." A stronghold is a mind-set that is filled with the hopelessness and despair that causes a person to accept as unchangeable something in their lives even though they know it goes contrary to the will of God.

It is within your mind that the devil has bound you into thinking that a certain situation is supposed to be a certain way and that there is no hope in it being any other way. But remember, as the Bible tells us in 2 Corinthians 4:7–12, "But we have this treasure in earthen vessels, that the excellency of the power may be of God, and not of us. We are troubled on every side, yet not distressed; we are perplexed, but not in despair; persecuted, but not forsaken; cast down, but not destroyed; always bearing about in the body the dying of the Lord Jesus, that the life also of Jesus might be made manifest in our body. For we which live are always delivered unto death for Jesus' sake, that the life also of Jesus might be made manifest in our mortal flesh. So then death worketh in us, but life in you."

John 8:36 says, "If the Son therefore shall make you free, ye shall be free indeed."

John 10:10 says, "The thief cometh not, but for to steal, and to kill, and to destroy: I am come that they might have life, and that they might have it more abundantly."

Spiritual warfare is a continuous battle that you must learn how to fight. If you don't war spiritually, you will be in bondage. In the natural war, there are casualties or lost lives for the enemy and the ones the war is coming against; however, in spiritual warfare, we have a guarantee that as long as we do the will of God, we will have everlasting life. Isaiah 54:17 tells us, "No weapon that is formed against thee shall prosper; and every tongue that shall rise against thee in judgment thou shalt condemn. This is the heritage of the servants of the Lord, and their righteousness is of me, saith the Lord."

If you want deliverance from bondage, you must change the way you think. It is terrible to allow the devil to control and waste your mind.

2. It is the world. God has sent us into the world as salt and light, but we are not of the world, which simply means we live in a hostile environment. We are just Christian soldiers passing through this

barren and tedious land. The world has its own agenda, its ideas, its ambitions, its usages, its aims; and these things are contrary to the mind of God. The world seeks to bring you under its sway, under its dominion, and it is our business to fight against that bondage.

First John 5:4 tells us, "For whatever is born of God overcomes the world; and this is the victory that has overcome the world our faith."

3. Flesh is also our enemy. Now, the physical flesh itself is not bad, because God made it and everything God made is good. So it is not the tangible flesh that is our enemy. It is the sinning nature of the flesh that is bad. For instance, the things we should not feed our bodies and do to our bodies or feed our minds we sometimes do anyway because of the struggle of that old sinning nature of the flesh.

4. Sin. When sin attacks us, we should fight it back. We don't need to yield to it for one second. If you are knocked down by it, you should jump right back up and fight the good fight. First John 1:9 says, "If we confess our sins, he is faithful and just to forgive us our sins, and to cleanse us from all unrighteousness." Don't be beaten down by sin; confess it, repent, and get up, and run the race. Second Timothy 2:5 tells us "that if anyone competes as an athlete, he does not win the prize unless he competes according to the rules." The rule for you is to confess your sins and to turn from them.

Fight the good fight in the name of Jesus.

Reflection

1. Read 2 Timothy 2:3–5 and tell how we can be a *single-minded* soldier of Christ Jesus.

_____

_____

_____

_____

_____

_____

2. What is the only way you can win the prize?

_____

_____

_____

_____

_____

_____

3. Read 2 Timothy 2:6 and discuss what it means to endure.

_____

_____

_____

_____

_____

_____

4. Read 2 Timothy 3:11 and state how Paul was rewarded for enduring.

_____

_____

_____

_____

_____

_____

5. Read John 6:27 and state what kind of nourishment you will need to endure and why.

_____

_____

_____

_____

_____

_____

6. What does 2 Corinthians 4:18 say are the real things?

_____

_____

_____

_____

_____

7. What does 1 Corinthians 3:14–18 say are the rewards?

_____

_____

_____

_____

_____

_____

_____

CHAPTER 20

It Is Time to Really Pray

Proverbs 15:29 tells us, "The LORD is far from the wicked: but he heareth the prayer of the righteous." Those who have not been born again are walking in a fallen state. They are unregenerate sinners existing as wicked unbelievers. The Holy One is far from them.

Their wickedness put a great distance between them and God. The only way one can get their prayers heard and answered is to be born again. You must accept Jesus as your Lord and Savior, be born again to be righteous. Jesus tells Nicodemus in John 3:7, "Ye must be born again." A spiritual birth must take place if you want to be justified.

Philippians 4:13 tells us, "I can do all things through Christ who strengthens me." It is through the strength of Jesus Christ that our prayers can do much. If you are saved, you are made righteous through the blood of Jesus. You are the righteous and you are called to pray.

In Matthew 7:7–11, Jesus instructs the people to ask, seek, and knock. He reveals to them that the ability to live for God is only a prayer away. He encourages them to never give up but to be consistent and persistent about their praying. It is only through prayer that believers can contact God, hear what God wants them to do, and acquire the strength to do God's will in all areas of their lives.

Why Pray?

- Prayer changes things.
- Prayer can get you wisdom. (James 1:5)
- Prayer can help you understand the word of God.
- Prayer can remove demonic barriers to harmony in your marriage, family, career, your happiness, and every situation you find yourself in.
- Prayer avails to bring the Holy Spirit in all His fullness, with all His graces and bestowments of power into our hearts and lives. (Luke 11:13)

It is time to really pray, because the black man and the black woman and their family are under final attack. The enemy knows his time is short and has set out to finish off the black family in particular. Now more than ever, he unleashes his rage and destruction against them. There are drive-by shootings, drugs, poverty, unemployment, and a high rate of divorce, among many other tragedies that plague the black community. It is really time to pray and subdue the enemies who have come to attack you and quench them as the fire of thorns. Isaiah 59:19 tells us, "So shall they fear the name of the LORD from the west, and his glory from the rising of the sun. When the enemy shall come in like a flood, the Spirit of the LORD shall lift up a standard against him."

It is time to really pray and then leave the battle to the Lord. You must pray and then just stand for the Lord. After you have done all you can do, you still just stand. You don't take matters into your own hands and try to figure out a man-made strategy, because it will not stand. God wants the glory in your deliverance.

In Exodus 14:7–14, the Bible says, "And he took six hundred chosen chariots and all the chariots of Egypt, and captains over every one of them. And the Lord hardened the heart of Pharaoh, King of Egypt, and he pursued after the children of Israel; and the children of Israel went out with a high hand. But the Egyptians pursued after all the horses and chariots of Pharaoh and his horsemen, and his army, and overtook them encamping by the sea, beside Pihahiroth, before Baalzephon. And when Pharaoh drew nigh, the children of Israel lifted up their eyes, and, behold, the Egyptians marched after them; and they were sore afraid: and the children of Israel cried out unto the LORD. And they said unto Moses: Because there were no graves in Egypt hast thou taken us away to die in the wilderness? Wherefore hast thou dealt thus with us, to carry us forth out of Egypt? Is not this the word that we did tell thee in Egypt, saying, Let us alone that we may serve the Egyptians? For it had been better for us to serve the Egyptians, than that we should die in the wilderness. And Moses said unto the people, Fear ye not, stand still, and see salvation of the LORD, which he will show to you today: for the Egyptians whom ye have seen today, ye shall see them again no more forever. The LORD shall fight for you and ye shall hold your peace."

Black men and black women, God does not want you to live in Doomsville, nor does He want you to get so comfortable with being down that you desire to stay down. Get up and fight for your marriage and your family by living according to God's will. Get up and fight by prevailing in prayer. This is no time to lose hope.

Families should pray together. "A family that prays together stays together."

In Matthew 18:19–20 Jesus says, "Again I say unto you, that if two of you agree on earth as touching anything that they shall ask, it shall be done for them of my Father which is in heaven." For where two or three are gathered together in my name, there am I in the midst of them." In the Greek the word, "agree" is *sumphoneo*. This is the same word in the English for "symphony." In a symphony a large number of instrumentalist work together to bring out the composer's work. Jesus is letting us know that our Father in heaven is our composer, and as we work together we can achieve the work of our Father in harmony. When you pray together, it will bring you closer to the person you are praying with because you can hear and agree with what comes out of their hearts. Praying together is an experience of unity and humility.

Your primary enemy is the devil, and you are his primary target. When you experience demonic attacks, you don't have to stand around helpless and defenseless.

Get up and fight back in prayer, and you will subdue the one that comes to attack you, if you are consistent and persistent. Isaiah 59:19 tells us, "So shall they fear the name of the LORD from the west, and his glory from the rising of the sun. When the enemy shall come in like a flood, the Spirit of the LORD shall lift up a standard against him." It is your responsibility to pray, and God will protect you from the enemy everywhere and in everything that concerns you. Never take things into your own hands because vengeance belongs to Lord. He is the only one that can really avenge for you. He is the only one that knows exactly what it is going to take to bring vengeance upon the devil. God is the only one that balance the scales for you in any and all aspects of your life. Why not talk to Him and give it to Him in prayer? The Bible says in James 4:7, "Submit yourselves therefore to God. Resists the devil, and he will flee from you." The only way to intimidate the enemy is to be a real spiritual warrior. You must use your weapons of warfare. Second Corinthians 10:4–5 tells us, "For the weapons of our warfare are not carnal, but mighty through God to the pulling down of strongholds; Casting down imaginations, and every high thing that exalteth itself against the knowledge of God, and bringing into captivity every thought to the obedience of Christ; and having in a readiness to revenge all disobedience, when your obedience is fulfilled." This cannot be done if you are walking according to the flesh or your worldly desires. You must walk in obedience to Christ, which can be seen in your actions, which will reveal your thoughts. In doing this you will be launching a counterattack against the enemy. In praying you must know and speak the word of God in the name of Jesus and by his blood. Bind the spirit of fear and every spirit that is in opposition to God. Psalm 46:10 tells us, "Be still, and know that I am God: I will be exalted among the heathen, I will be exalted in the earth." The one and only Almighty God has the final say and final judgment. He is the commander of all things, and He will be exalted, and all will bow before Him. You are a guaranteed winner if you are on His team and if you obey His commandments and follow His instructions in prayer. The enemy must halt and surrender his attack against you as you stand and fight against the enemy in the name of Jesus and by His Blood. Then your prayers will bring deliverance to you wholly. Every crooked way will be made straight and every rotten area of your life and every affliction must flee from you if you will pray fervently from a clean heart. In Obadiah 1:17, the Bible says, "Upon Mount Zion, there shall be deliverance and there shall be holiness and the house of Jacob shall possess their possessions." There will be judgment on God's enemies and blessings on God's people. The devil never gives up, and you should never give up. Spiritual warfare is an ongoing battle, and you must learn to keep fighting. You cannot afford to become complacent or lazy in a war, because if you do, the enemy will walk all over you. It can be seen as suicidal for anyone to know that they are in the line of fire and just stand there and let it come up on them. In a natural war, many lives will be lost from both sides. But in a spiritual war, you are guaranteed that as long as you do the will of God, you will have everlasting life. Isaiah 54:17 says, "No weapon that is formed against thee shall prosper; and every tongue that shall rise against thee in judgment thou shalt condemn. This is the heritage of the servants of the Lord, and their righteousness is of me, saith the Lord." If your righteousness is of God, you will not fulfill the lust of the flesh. You will not fall into the pride of life, nor will you succumb to the lust of the eye. You will continue to walk in deliverance.

The Requirements to Live a Delivered Life

1. *You must be born again to wage war against the devil.*

2. *Repent of your sins and ask God to forgive you.* Name each known sin and confess it. Also confess all unknown sins and sins of omission and commission. Ask the Lord to cleanse you with the blood He shed on the cross at Calvary for the remission of your sins. Ask the Lord to come into your heart and live His life in you as you live your life through Him. Get off the throne of your life and let Him be on the throne of your life and make Him the Lord of your life as well as your Savior. Surrender your life to Him completely and follow Him with all your heart. Turn away from the world and the devil and be set apart for His purposes only. Now you can say as Paul said in Philippians 4:13, *"I can do all things through Christ who strengthens me."* The Lord will secure you and uphold you with His hand of righteousness, and you will be able to stand against the wiles of the devil, in the name of Jesus. Now you have the privilege of making your pharaoh sink in the Red Sea and rise above your oppressors.

Reflection

- The Bible tells us in James 5:16 what kind of prayer that is effective.

    Good prayer is talking to God. Good prayer is taking the time to be still and listen to God. Sometimes we talk too much when we need to listen to the divine heartbeat of our living God. We should want our time in prayer to be a wise investment and not just a time of beating air. The only way our prayer is going to be of any effect is if it comes out of righteousness. James 5:16c says, "The effectual fervent prayer of a righteous man availeth much." Good prayer needs to arise out of the heart, not just the mouth. There are principles we must follow to have effective prayer.

The Principles of Prayer

1. Principle of a *pure heart*: Psalm 66:18 tells you that your heart must be _____.

First Samuel 14:37 and 1 Samuel 28:6 tells us that we

_____

_____

_____

_____

2. Principle of a *forgiving spirit*: Bitterness and anger are growing in churches, homes, and schools, and in the world as a whole. See Colossians 3:19, 1 Peter 3:7, Mark 11:25–26.

_____

_____

_____

_____

_____

3. Principle of *faith*: Don't pray a lot of words and then worry. Worry is a type of doubt. Doubt is a type of fear. This will not happen if you pray until you get a breakthrough. See Hebrews 11:6, Mark 11:23.

_____

_____

_____

_____

_____

4. Principle of *right motive*: Anyone with a spirit of dishonesty will pray selfishly.
   See James 4:3.

_____

_____

_____

_____

_____

5. Principle of *God's will*: See 1 John 5:14: "Thy will be done on earth as it is in heaven." Seek His will and you will never pray incorrectly.

_____

_____

_____

_____

_____

6. Principle of the Law of *Jesus's name*: See John 14:14: Jesus's stamp must be on the mail in order for it to be accepted.

_____

_____

_____

_____

_____

Principle of praying in the *Spirit*: When we yield to God's Spirit, we can pray more effectively. See Jude 1:20.

_____

_____

_____

_____

_____

Study the effective prayers of some of the saints.

Teachers of Prayer: Jesus in Matthew 6:5–15, Paul in Philippians 4:6 Fill in the blank with the name of the one prayed for and the results below:

1. 1 Samuel 1:11_____

2. 2 Kings 19:14–19; 20:1–11_____

3. Jonah 2:1–10._____

4. Ezra 8:21–23_____

5. Genesis 18:23–33_____

6. Nehemiah 1:5–11_____

7. Exodus 32:1–35_____

8. Psalm 99:6_____

9. 1 Kings 18:24–38_____

10. 2 Kings 1:10–12_____

7. How do these effective prayers effect how you will pray for the rest of your life?

_____

_____

_____

_____

_____

The same thing God did for these saints he can do for you too. It is time to pray! Pray to the only one who can help!

Bibliography

Anderson, Neil T. and Terry E. Zuehlke and Julianne S. Zuehlke. *Christ Centered Therapy*. Grand Rapids, Michigan: Zondervan Publishing House, 2000.

Barton, Bruce and Phillip Comfort and Grant Osborne and Linda K. Taylor and Dave Veerman. *Life Application New Testament Commentary*. Wheaton, Illinois: Tyndale House Publishers, Inc., 2001.

Blackwell, James E. *The Black Community Diversity and Unity*. New York, NY: Harper & Row Publishers Inc., 1975.

Carlson, Dwight L. *Overcoming Hurts & Anger*. Eugene, Oregon: Harvest House Publishers, 1981.

Clarke, Adam. *Adam Clarke Commentary*. 6 vols. PC Study Bible, Version 2. IJ. CD Rom. Seattle, Washington: Biblesoft, 1993–1998.

Draper, James T. Jr. Say Neighbor-Your House is on Fire! Dallas, Texas: Crescendo Book Publications, 1975.

DuBois, W.E.B. *Black Reconstruction In America*. New York: Atheneum, 1932, 1962.

Erickson, Gerald D. and Terrence P. Hogan. *Family Therapy 2nd edition*. Belmont, California: Brooks/Cole Publishing Company, Wadsworth, Inc.

Henry, Matthew. *Matthew Henry's Commentary.* 6 vols. PC Study Bible, Version 2.1JCD Rom. Seattle, Washington: Biblesoft, 1993–1998.

Hemfelt, Robert and Frank Minirth and Paul Meier. *Love IS A Choice.* Nashville, Tennessee: Thomas Nelson, Inc., Publishers, 1989.

Horton, Paul and Chester L. Hunt. *Sociology, 3rd edition.* Western Michigan University: McGraw Hills, 1972.

Landis, Paul H. *Making The Most of Marriage, 4th edition.* New York, N.Y.: Meredith Corporation, 1970.

Redding, Saunders. *They Came in Chains.* Philadelphia: J. B. Lippincott Company, 1950, 1973.

Sherrer, Quin and Ruthanne Garlock. *A Woman's Guide to Breaking Bondages.* Ann Arbor, Michigan: Servant Publications, 1994.

Strong's Exhaustive Concordance of the Bible. PC Study Bible, Version 2.1J CD Rom. Seattle, Washington: Biblesoft, 1993–1998.

Unger, Merril F. *Unger's Commentary on the Old Testament.* Chattanooga, TN: AMG Publishers, 2002.

Will, George F. "Defending Black Incarceration Rates." *Pittsburgh Tribune-Review* (June 2008): 2.

Zodhiates, Spiros. *The Hebrew-Greek Key Study Bible.* Chattanooga, Tennessee: AMG Publishers, 1991.

http://en.wikipedia.org/wiki/Fredrick _ Douglass http://en.wikipedia.org/wiki/James Cash Penny

About the Author

Dr. Christine Ainer is cofounder and copastor of Evangequip Missions Bible Fellowship Church in Hemet, California, with her husband, Bishop Leon K. Ainer Jr. She is also cofounder and president of Evangequip Missions Bible College and Seminary, founded in January 13, 2012.

She has ministered to women in an effort to mobilize them upwardly as well as counseled abandoned abused women and children for over twenty-nine years. Her goal is to encourage them to look to God and depend on him and his guidance for everything in life.

She earned a Bachelor of Arts degree in sociology from California State University Dominquez Hills, a Master of Divinity, from Golden Gate Baptist Theological Seminary in Brea, California.

She also earned a Doctorate of Ministry.